COCHISE

COCHISE
Apache Chief

Melissa Schwarz

Senior Consulting Editor
W. David Baird
Howard A. White Professor of History
Pepperdine University

CHELSEA HOUSE PUBLISHERS

New York   Philadelphia

FRONTISPIECE   A late-19th-century photograph of the entrance to
Cochise's hideout in the Dragoon Mountains.

ON THE COVER   This portrait of Cochise was painted after an 1884
photograph of his son Naiche, who is said to have closely resembled his
father. There exists no known photograph of Cochise or portrait of the
leader made during his lifetime.

Chelsea House Publishers
EDITOR-IN-CHIEF   Remmel Nunn
MANAGING EDITOR   Karyn Gullen Browne
COPY CHIEF   Mark Rifkin
PICTURE EDITOR   Adrian G. Allen
ART DIRECTOR   Maria Epes
ASSISTANT ART DIRECTOR   Howard Brotman
MANUFACTURING DIRECTOR   Gerald Levine
SYSTEMS MANAGER   Lindsey Ottman
PRODUCTION MANAGER   Joseph Romano
PRODUCTION COORDINATOR   Marie Claire Cebrián

North American Indians of Achievement
SENIOR EDITOR   Liz Sonneborn

Staff for COCHISE
ASSISTANT EDITOR   Leigh Hope Wood
COPY EDITOR   Christopher Duffy
EDITORIAL ASSISTANT   Michele Berezansky
DESIGNER   Debora Smith
PICTURE RESEARCHER   Vicky Haluska
COVER ILLUSTRATION   Danny O'Leary

3   5   7   9   8   6   4

Library of Congress Cataloging-in-Publication Data

Schwarz, Melissa
Cochise—Apache Chief/by Melissa Schwarz
p. cm.—(North American Indians of achievement)
Includes index.
Summary: Examines the life and career of the noted Apache warrior chief.
ISBN 0-7910-1706-0
0-7910-1694-3 (pbk.)
1. Cochise, Apache chief, d. 1874—Juvenile literature. 2. Apache Indians—Biog-
raphy—Juvenile literature. [1. Cochise, Apache chief, d. 1874. 2. Apache Indians—
Biography. 3. Indians of North America—Biography.] I. Title. II. Series
E99.A6C576 1992   91-23495
973'.0497202—dc20   CIP
[B]   AC

CONTENTS

NORTH AMERICAN INDIANS OF ACHIEVEMENT

BLACK HAWK
Sac Rebel

JOSEPH BRANT
Mohawk Chief

COCHISE
Apache Chief

CRAZY HORSE
Sioux War Chief

CHIEF GALL
Sioux War Chief

GERONIMO
Apache Warrior

HIAWATHA
Founder of the Iroquois
Confederacy

CHIEF JOSEPH
Nez Perce Leader

PETER MACDONALD
Former Chairman of the Navajo
Nation

WILMA MANKILLER
Principal Chief of the Cherokees

OSCEOLO
Seminole Rebel

QUANAH PARKER
Comanche Chief

KING PHILIP
Wampanoag Rebel

POCAHONTAS AND CHIEF POWHATAN
Leaders of the Powhatan Tribes

PONTIAC
Ottawa Rebel

RED CLOUD
Sioux War Chief

WILL ROGERS
Cherokee Entertainer

SEQUOYAH
Inventor of the Cherokee Alphabet

SITTING BULL
Chief of the Sioux

TECUMSEH
Shawnee Rebel

JIM THORPE
Sac and Fox Athlete

SARAH WINNEMUCCA
Northern Paiute Writer and
Diplomat

Other titles in preparation

ON INDIAN LEADERSHIP

by W. David Baird

Howard A. White Professor of History

Pepperdine University

Authoritative utterance is in thy mouth, perception is in thy heart, and thy tongue is the shrine of justice," the ancient Egyptians said of their king. From him, the Egyptians expected authority, discretion, and just behavior. Homer's *Iliad* suggests that the Greeks demanded somewhat different qualities from their leaders: justice and judgment, wisdom and counsel, shrewdness and cunning, valor and action. It is not surprising that different people living at different times should seek different qualities from the individuals they looked to for guidance. By and large, a people's requirements for leadership are determined by two factors: their culture and the unique circumstances of the time and place in which they live.

Before the late 15th century, when non-Indians first journeyed to what is now North America, most Indian tribes were not ruled by a single person. Instead, there were village chiefs, clan headmen, peace chiefs, war chiefs, and a host of other types of leaders, each with his or her own specific duties. These influential people not only decided political matters but also helped shape their tribe's social, cultural, and religious life. Usually, Indian leaders held their positions because they had won the respect of their peers. Indeed, if a leader's followers at any time decided that he or she was out of step with the will of the people, they felt free to look to someone else for advice and direction.

Thus, the greatest achievers in traditional Indian communities were men and women of extraordinary talent. They were not only skilled at navigating the deadly waters of tribal politics and cultural customs but also able to, directly or indirectly, make a positive and significant difference in the daily life of their followers.

From the beginning of their interaction with Native Americans, non-Indians failed to understand these features of Indian leadership. Early European explorers and settlers merely assumed that Indians had the same relationship with their leaders as non-Indians had with their kings and queens. European monarchs generally inherited their positions and ruled large nations however they chose, often with little regard for the desires or needs of their subjects. As a result, the settlers of Jamestown saw Pocahontas as a "princess" and Pilgrims dubbed Wampanoag leader Metacom "King Philip," envisioning them in roles very different from those in which their own people placed them.

As more and more non-Indians flocked to North America, the nature of Indian leadership gradually began to change. Influential Indians no longer had to take on the often considerable burden of pleasing only their own people; they also had to develop a strategy of dealing with the non-Indian newcomers. In a rapidly changing world, new types of Indian role models with new ideas and talents continually emerged. Some were warriors; others were peacemakers. Some held political positions within their tribes; others were writers, artists, religious prophets, or athletes. Although the demands of Indian leadership altered from generation to generation, several factors that determined which Indian people became prominent in the centuries after first contact remained the same.

Certain personal characteristics distinguished these Indians of achievement. They were intelligent, imaginative, practical, daring, shrewd, uncompromising, ruthless, and logical. They were constant in friendships, unrelenting in hatreds, affectionate with their relatives, and respectful to their God or gods. Of course, no single Native American leader embodied all these qualities, nor these qualities only. But it was these characteristics that allowed them to succeed.

The special skills and talents that certain Indians possessed also brought them to positions of importance. The life of Hiawatha, the legendary founder of the powerful Iroquois Confederacy, displays the value that oratorical ability had for many Indians in power.

The biography of Cochise, the 19th-century Apache chief, illustrates that leadership often required keen diplomatic skills not only in transactions among tribespeople but also in hardheaded negotiations with non-Indians. For others, such as Mohawk Joseph Brant and Navajo Peter MacDonald, a non-Indian education proved advantageous in their dealings with other peoples.

Sudden changes in circumstance were another crucial factor in determining who became influential in Indian communities. King Philip in the 1670s and Geronimo in the 1880s both came to power when their people were searching for someone to lead them into battle against white frontiersmen who had forced upon them a long series of indignities. Seeing the rising discontent of Indians of many tribes in the 1810s, Tecumseh and his brother, the Shawnee prophet Tenskwatawa, proclaimed a message of cultural revitalization that appealed to thousands. Other Indian achievers recognized cooperation with non-Indians as the most advantageous path during their lifetime. Sarah Winnemucca in the late 19th century bridged the gap of understanding between her people and their non-Indian neighbors through the publication of her autobiography *Life Among the Piutes*. Olympian Jim Thorpe in the early 20th century championed the assimilationist policies of the U.S. government and, with his own successes, demonstrated the accomplishments Indians could make in the non-Indian world. And Wilma Mankiller, principal chief of the Cherokees, continues to fight successfully for the rights of her people through the courts and through negotiation with federal officials.

Leadership among Native Americans, just as among all other peoples, can be understood only in the context of culture and history. But the centuries that Indians have had to cope with invasions of foreigners in their homelands have brought unique hardships and obstacles to the Native American individuals who most influenced and inspired others. Despite these challenges, there has never been a lack of Indian men and women equal to these tasks. With such strong leaders, it is no wonder that Native Americans remain such a vital part of this nation's cultural landscape.

1

SHATTERED TRUST: THE CUT THE TENT AFFAIR

Cochise's wife Dos-teh-seh, shown here in about 1885, was released on February 19, 1861, from U.S. custody. With her son Naiche, she returned to the Chiricahuas unharmed, but Cochise was led to believe, probably by Dos-teh-seh, that a card game had decided their fate.

High in the Dos Cabezas mountains, in present-day Arizona, Cochise, the chief of the Chiricahua Apaches, waited patiently for James Wallace to catch his breath. Gathered nearby were members of Cochise's family, who were also eager to hear what the white man had to say. Chiricahua scouts had seen American soldiers camped below at Apache Pass, and Cochise wished to find out why the soldiers had come.

There were few settlers in Chiricahua territory in February 1861, but Cochise had grown used to American travelers and military personnel stopping at Apache Pass. The freshwater spring at the pass offered the only water for miles around, and in 1858, Cochise had allowed the Butterfield Overland Mail Company to build a rest station there. Not long afterward the Butterfield Company began its twice weekly mail route along the California Trail. For more than two years stagecoaches carrying mail and passengers had traveled the trail in safety.

Wallace drank some water offered by Cochise's wife, then delivered his message in Apache: American military officer Second Lieutenant George Bascom wished to discuss some missing cattle and a boy who had been taken from a ranch about 50 miles away. John Ward, the boy's stepfather, was waiting with Bascom at Apache Pass. They wanted to talk to Cochise.

Cochise was tall for an Apache—almost six feet—and most of the American officers who came in contact with him were impressed by his appearance. He had an attractive face—a high forehead, strong cheekbones, and a straight nose—and, in traditional Apache style, he wore his jet black hair, which was streaked with gray, to his shoulders. Most notable, the chief carried himself with authority. One officer reported that he stood "straight as an arrow, built, from the ground up, as perfect as a man could be." Another described him as "powerful and exceedingly well-built." And still another commented that his "countenance displayed great force of character."

In 1861, the chief was about 55 years old. He was a strong, intelligent man with gentle manners, and he was an unusually powerful Apache leader. The son of a chief, he had been trained to lead from a young age. The whites who knew him both feared and respected him, and in general, most considered him to be a man of his word. But Bascom knew almost nothing of Cochise's reputation and could see very little beyond his own desire to succeed at his first mission.

At Fort Buchanan, where John Ward had reported his boy missing, Bascom's superior officer had ordered Bascom to use whatever means necessary to recover the child, and he was determined to do so. Starting out from Ward's ranch, Bascom and 54 of his men followed the Indian trail as best they could. They guessed the trail led to Cochise's mountains, and although Bascom had never met the chief of the Chiricahuas, he was sure the mighty Apache was hiding the boy. He camped near the Butterfield station and sent Wallace to bring the chief down out of the mountains, telling him that he wished only to question Cochise so as not to alert the Indian to his plans.

Lieutenant George Bascom, who had no experience dealing with Indians, received orders on January 29, 1861, from his superior officer at Fort Buchanan to pursue those who were responsible for raiding John Ward's ranch and taking a young boy captive.

Because the Chiricahua warriors were not responsible for the raid on Ward's ranch, Cochise naturally assumed that the soldiers camped below had come in peace, seeking information. He came down to meet with them around dinner time, with his brother, Coyuntura; his wife, Dos-teh-seh; his young son Naiche; and two nephews. That he came with his family was a sign of trust. But Lieutenant Bascom had no experience dealing with Indians, and he did not recognize the sign or heed its meaning.

After the usual greetings, Bascom invited Cochise and
the other warriors into his tent to eat and drink. When
the chief and his relatives had been made comfortable,
Bascom began to question Cochise about the raid, using
Ward as an interpreter. Cochise told Bascom that the
Chiricahuas were not involved in the incident. In his
opinion the boy had been taken by the White Mountain
Apaches, a band to the north of the Chiricahuas that had
a reputation for taking captives. Cochise explained that

*The ruins of the Ward ranch on
Sonoita Creek, located 11 miles
south of Fort Buchanan. The
day after John Ward reported
that his stepson had been taken
by Apaches, Lieutenant Bascom
examined the trail leading from
the ranch and determined, incor-
rectly, that Cochise's band was
responsible.*

although he did not have power over the other band, if Bascom wished it he would do what he could to help recover the child. (Years later, it turned out that Cochise was correct. After living with the White Mountain Apaches, the boy returned as an adult named Mickey Free and, with his knowledge of the Apache language, became an interpreter for the U.S. military.)

While Cochise talked, one of Bascom's men slipped out and told the other soldiers to surround the tent. Bascom was convinced that Cochise had the boy, and he did not intend to go back to Fort Buchanan empty-handed. As soon as he knew his men were in place, Bascom flatly accused Cochise of lying.

At first Cochise did not understand the American soldier. He thought perhaps he was making a joke. Then Bascom informed Cochise through Ward that Cochise and his relatives would be held prisoner until both the cattle and the boy were returned, and the smile dropped from the chief's face.

Shocked and furious, Cochise reacted quickly. He stood up, pulled his knife from its sheath on his leg, slashed a hole in the tent, and escaped. The soldiers outside were taken completely by surprise. It took them several seconds to collect themselves, giving Cochise more than enough time to speed past them and up a nearby hill. When he was near the top, a bullet caught him in the leg, but it did not stop him. Cochise later told an American that he ran all the way up the hill with his coffee cup still in his hand.

One of Cochise's nephews was not so lucky. He too leaped through the hole in the tent, but the soldiers were ready for him. They clubbed him fiercely, and one stuck him to the ground with a bayonet. The other Indians never had a chance. They sat quietly inside the tent, having become Bascom's prisoners.

Over the next few days, Cochise tried hard to convince Bascom that he was innocent. His family meant the world to him, and he would do everything he could to get them back. The morning after he escaped from the tent, Cochise appeared on the hill with a white flag and sent an unarmed warrior to inform Bascom that he wished to talk. Bascom met the chief and three warriors at the appointed place with an equal number of men. One of the soldiers at the meeting, Sergeant Daniel Robinson, later reported that Cochise tried to convince Bascom that he did not have the boy and pleaded for the release of his relatives. Bascom responded that they "would be set free just so soon as the boy [is] restored."

Just as the meeting was ending, James Wallace, Charles Culver, and a third Butterfield employee left the stage station against Bascom's orders. Unlike the young lieutenant, they understood that falsely accusing the Apaches was serious business, and they hoped to reason with the Indians before the matter got out of hand. But the damage had already been done. The Indians no longer trusted the Butterfield men. When the three men emerged, the Indians immediately ran for cover and opened fire. Wallace was taken hostage by the Apaches; Culver was shot in the back but carried to safety; and the third employee, who was accidentally mistaken for an Indian as he ran back toward the station through the trees, was killed by an American soldier.

The following day, Sergeant Robinson led a herd of cattle to drink at the spring, which was about 600 yards from the station. The Americans had anticipated a fight, but Cochise merely watched from the hill overlooking the station. He was not interested in the cattle. Cattle would not help him recover his relatives.

According to Robinson, the Apaches appeared on the hill a couple of hours later, leading Wallace, who had

After he was abducted by the White Mountain Apaches, John Ward's stepson, later known as Mickey Free, lived among the Indians all his life and became a scout and interpreter for the U.S. Army. He died on the Fort Apache Reservation in 1915.

"his arms bound behind his back, and a rope around his neck." The chief again asked Bascom to free his family and offered to give him Wallace and some mules in exchange. Wallace pleaded with Bascom to make the trade, shouting that he himself would find the boy. But by this time, it seemed that Bascom was beyond reasoning. In fact, the offer to exchange Wallace, who had disobeyed his orders in the first place, seemed to anger him more. He remained adamant, saying that he would trade only if the Ward boy were included in the deal.

Cochise's concern for his family and frustration at being held responsible for a crime he did not commit grew stronger and led him to act out of anger and desperation. That evening, veteran driver José Antonio Montoya, a Mexican, led five wagons toward Apache Pass on the way to a town in Mexico. Each wagon carted a full load of flour, and one carried three American passengers. Montoya had made the trip many times, and because the Apaches had allowed travelers to pass in safety for more than two years, he had no reason to suspect trouble. Even if he had, there would have been little he could do. As the wagons climbed the trail toward the stage station, a small band of Cochise's warriors attacked them. The Mexicans, who were longtime enemies of the Apaches, were tied to the wagon wheels. Then the wheels were set on fire. The three Americans were taken prisoner.

That night, Cochise instructed Wallace to write a message to Bascom saying, "Treat my people well and I will do the same by yours, of whom I have four." The note was fastened to a bush near Bascom's camp. But the lieutenant did not find it until two days later, and by then it was too late.

The next day was just like any other to the eastbound Butterfield stage driver making his way along the trail.

The last thing he expected was an Apache attack. Then, suddenly, two shots rang out. The driver was wounded, and one of the mules pulling the stage was killed. William Buckley, the superintendent of the route, just happened to be riding in the stage. He jumped out, pulled the driver inside, cut loose the dead mule, and took the reins himself.

About a mile down the road, he saw the bodies of the Mexicans still smoldering and began to whip the remaining mules. Up ahead he could see that the Apaches had torn away part of a small stone bridge used to cross a ravine. Determined to reach the station, Buckley forced the mules to jump the bridge, and somehow the stage's momentum carried it across. He arrived at the station around two o'clock the next morning. Robinson recalled that "everything around us was as still as a graveyard that night."

Because Bascom had not responded to Cochise's note, the chief assumed that he refused to trade hostages. By attacking the stage, Cochise had hoped to capture more Americans to exchange for the Apaches held by Bascom. Now the only choice left to him was to rescue his family by force.

One of the first things Cochise had done after escaping from Bascom's tent was to send a messenger to Dos-teh-seh's father, Mangas Coloradas, the great chief of the Mimbreno Apaches. It was not unusual for an Apache leader to enlist the help of another leader, and the ties between Cochise and Mangas were especially tight. Mangas was an enormous man—six feet four inches tall—and like Cochise, his great courage and skill as a warrior had earned him influence that extended beyond his own band. Mangas arrived with more than 200 warriors, who promptly joined the Chiricahuas. If Bascom would not see reason, Cochise would see him dead.

That night, the Americans at Apache Pass saw "signal fires blazing from the peaks" and heard drums and

Apache Pass in Arizona Territory, photographed by William A. Bell, circa 1867. In Cochise's day, the freshwater spring at the pass was the only source of water for miles around; until the Cut the Tent affair, Americans could use it in relative safety.

shouting. The combined bands were probably performing a war dance reserved only for major battles. In such cases a war shaman led the ceremony, calling on Usen, the Apache god, to bring the warriors success in battle. Then when the sky was dark, the Apaches lit a large fire. As flames rose and sparks flew up into the sky, one of the warriors beat a drum. Each individual warrior stepped forward and danced or simply walked around the fire to show his commitment to the war party. Other tribe members left the camp and went into the surrounding mountains to pray for strength against the enemy. The ceremony continued until just before sunrise.

Cochise planned his attack well, but success depended on Bascom's reaction. Every day the station's cattle and mules were taken to the spring to drink. According to

COCHISE'S RANGE (1821–1874)

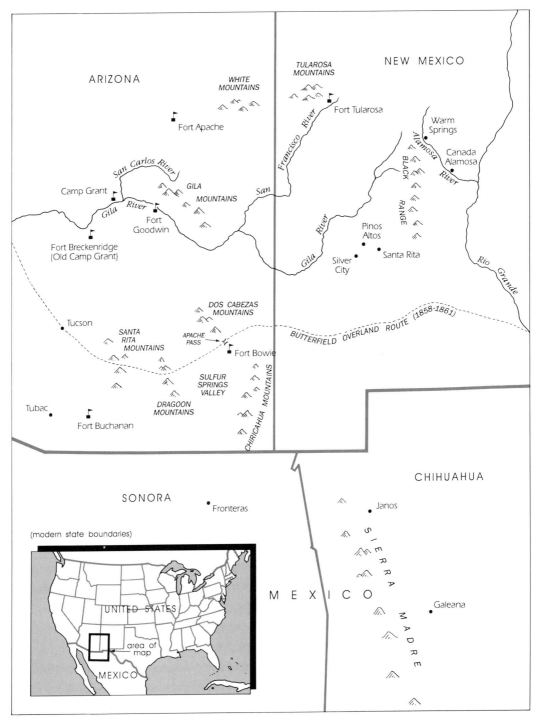

ARIZONA

NEW MEXICO

WHITE
MOUNTAINS

TULAROSA
MOUNTAINS

Fort Tularosa

Warm
Springs

Canada
Alamosa

Fort Apache

San Carlos River

GILA
MOUNTAINS

Camp Grant

Gila River

Fort
Goodwin

Fort Breckenridge
(Old Camp Grant)

Francisco River

San

Gila River

BLACK RANGE

Alamosa River

Pinos
Altos

Silver
City

Santa Rita

Rio Grande

Tucson

DOS CABEZAS
MOUNTAINS

SANTA
RITA
MOUNTAINS

APACHE
PASS

Fort Bowie

BUTTERFIELD OVERLAND ROUTE (1858-1861)

SULFUR
SPRINGS
VALLEY

Tubac

Fort Buchanan

DRAGOON
MOUNTAINS

CHIRICAHUA MOUNTAINS

CHIHUAHUA

SONORA

Fronteras

Janos

(modern state boundaries)

SIERRA MADRE

UNITED STATES

area of
map

MEXICO

M E X I C O

Galeana

Cochise's plan, the Apaches would wait until the herd was at the spring and ambush it, drawing the soldiers out from the station. A second group of warriors would then attack the unprotected station and retrieve the hostages.

On the morning of the attack, Robinson was with the herd of animals. He later recorded what he saw:

> A large party of Apaches [came down the mountains] moving at a swinging gait. They were in war dress, naked and painted, and they were singing a war song. They were coming so open and boldly that they no doubt expected to sweep all before them without much trouble. We opened fire at once, [and] forced them to change their course so as to leave the way open to the station.

As it happened, Bascom sent only a few of his soldiers out to the battle at the spring and allowed the Apaches to take most of the cattle. When Cochise and his second line of warriors attacked the station house, they were quickly beaten back by the soldiers, who could shoot from under cover. The Apache rescue attempt was over quickly. Cochise accepted the fact that he might not see his family again and ordered his people to leave for Mexico. Consumed with hatred, he allowed his warriors to torture the four American prisoners to death.

Believing themselves surrounded, Bascom and his men stayed in the vicinity of the station for three days. Then reinforcements under Lieutenant Isaiah Moore arrived from Fort Breckenridge, and a scouting party was organized. Moore and Bascom led a company of 110 men into the mountains but did not find a single Apache. What they did find were the bodies of the four Americans—Wallace and the three stage passengers. All were mutilated beyond recognition.

The sight was so horrible that soon everyone at the station—military and civilians alike—began to call for the execution of the Apache hostages. Some of the witnesses said later that Bascom resisted the idea, arguing that Cochise's family should be treated as prisoners of war. But Lieutenant Moore insisted on their execution and said he would assume full responsibility.

The following morning at dawn, Bascom and Moore left the station to return to their home forts, taking the Indians with them. As they rode through the pass, Bascom asked the interpreter to explain their intentions to the Apaches. The warriors asked to be shot instead of hanged, and they requested whiskey. Both requests were denied. Coyuntura and Cochise's two nephews then accepted their fate and, according to Robinson, "sang their death songs." The soldiers hung Cochise's relatives in the same spot where they had buried the Americans, under four oak trees that stood in a row just above the trail. They left their bodies swinging in the wind.

Dos-teh-seh and her young son, Naiche, were taken to Fort Breckenridge and released. But what the Americans would later call the Cochise Wars had already begun. Cochise had tried to be reasonable with the Americans even though they accused him unjustly. He had offered to help Bascom find the boy, and he had taken prisoners only because he hoped to trade them for his relatives. A few years later, Cochise said of the affair, "I was at peace with the whites until they tried to kill me for what other Indians did; I now live and die at war with them."

Although this legendary incident lasted only two weeks, it resulted in a full decade of revenge by the Apaches and terror for the American citizens living in the territory that is now Arizona and New Mexico. Over the next few months, word of the Cut the Tent affair frightened the Americans, and for many, the small forts that peppered the Chiricahuas' territory could offer no protection.

Together, Cochise and Mangas Coloradas decided that the time had come to drive the "white eyes" from their

This drawing of Indians attacking a Butterfield Overland coach was printed in Harper's Weekly in 1866. When the Butterfield Company began carrying passengers and mail between St. Louis and San Francisco in September 1858, Cochise was still at peace with the Americans. After Bascom's treachery at Apache Pass, the road through the heart of Chiricahua country became the most dangerous section of the route.

homelands. Operating out of his mountain stronghold, Cochise sent bands of warriors to attack wagon trains, stampede cattle, and murder settlers. The U.S. military had no hope of controlling them. The Apaches knew every trail, canyon, and water source for hundreds of miles. They could travel on foot over the roughest mountains and mesas, and when the soldiers were lucky enough to get close, they could disappear behind rocks, cacti, and tufts of bear grass.

Within a few weeks, nearly 150 stagecoach drivers, ranchers, and miners were killed in Apache raids. Some of them had had no idea that the peace they had enjoyed for two years had come to an end.

2

SON OF A CHIRICAHUA CHIEF

A drawing made by L. Linati in 1828 of an Apache chief. Most Apache legends claim that Cochise descended from a long line of chiefs, and though he was expected to follow in their footsteps, he could not simply inherit the leadership role. According to Apache tradition, only through his own accomplishments and show of wisdom could a chief's son ascend to his father's position.

Long before Cochise was born, the Apaches had encountered a people who were obsessed with legends of hidden gold and precious stones. These men had traveled north through Mexico, destroying or claiming all that lay in their path. When they first met the Apaches, around 1590, they viewed these Indians as only a minor threat and determined that they would make good slaves. With this objective in mind, they hunted the Indians mercilessly, using scalping and torture to frighten them into submission.

As they colonized Mexico, these people took the life or freedom of many Apaches. But in time the Indians rallied their forces and fought back, adopting the gruesome practices used by their new enemies—the Spanish conquistadores. Apache raids on Spanish settlements were swift and violent. Before long the invaders realized they had made a terrible enemy.

The balance of power in the war between the Spanish and the Apaches shifted many times over the next 200 years. By the 1790s, the Spaniards had grown tired of combat with the Apaches and decided to try a more devious strategy. They began to offer the Indians free food and clothing, along with plenty of alcohol, as a way of controlling Apache raids. Their intention was to make the Indians dependent on these gifts, to soften them and make them weak. Some Mexican officials even went so far as to give the Indians guns for hunting, hoping they would forget how to use their bows and arrows. As part of the plan, the guns were broken so that the Apaches would have to rely on Spanish blacksmiths to repair them. To be eligible to receive these "gifts," the Indians were required to live in designated areas near military forts, called *presidios*, that were scattered throughout northern Mexico. This system continued off and on for nearly 30 years, although at times the Apaches' rations were cut short because of a lack of funds. When Cochise was born, in approximately 1805, the presidio system was still in effect. In spite of this system, Cochise had a traditional Apache upbringing. His family did not stay near presidios year-round. Like most of the Apaches, they returned to their native territory whenever possible to hunt and gather wild foods. The temporary break in hostilities with the Spanish made life more stable for the young Cochise.

The Chiricahuas were one of several Apache bands that lived in the Southwest in what is now southern Arizona and New Mexico. Although there were strong ties between the bands, with much visiting and intermarriage, each band was a separate cultural group, with its own territory and its own leaders.

Chiricahua territory, where Cochise was born, included the rocky Dragoon, Dos Cabezas, and Chiricahua mountains—some of the roughest, most awesome mountains in the region. To the east of the Chiricahuas lived the Mimbreno Apaches, known later among the Americans as the Coppermines because copper and gold were discovered on their homeland. The Chihenne, or Warm Springs, Apaches, who got their name from a bathing pool and spring above the Alamosa River, lived to the east of the Mimbrenos. To the north of the Chiricahuas

An Apache woman with a baby. To protect a newborn Apache from bad forces, a shaman attached bags of pollen or the claw of a hummingbird to the baby's cradle.

were a small band called the Bedonkohes. To the south, in the Sierra Madre, lived the Nednhis. Members of each of these bands would play important roles in Cochise's life.

Each Apache band was divided into local groups, and each group consisted of several extended families who lived together in camps known as rancherías. Each group also had its own leaders, although the powerful one, as Cochise would one day become, had influence outside of their groups and even outside of their bands.

That the Apaches did not keep written records and considered talking about the dead taboo has made it difficult for historians to reconstruct Cochise's family history. His mother's name is not known, and the identity of his father remains a mystery. There is strong evidence that Cochise was the son of Pisago Cabezón, a Chiricahua Apache chief who came to power in the 1830s. But most Apache legends simply say that Cochise descended from a long line of chiefs and was raised to follow in their footsteps.

Although Apache leaders did not inherit their positions but rather earned them by demonstrating their abilities and influencing others, the son of a great chief was treated specially and had a good chance to become a leader himself. Ceremonies and rituals accompanied every stage of an Apache's life—from birth to death. When Cochise was about four days old (a magical number to the Apaches), a *shaman*, or medicine man, would have constructed a cradle for him, known as a *tsoch*, and attached bags of pollen or the claw of a hummingbird to protect him from bad forces. When Cochise learned to walk, another ceremony would celebrate his first pair of

A Chiricahua Apache camp on the San Carlos River in Arizona, circa 1883. Each time the Apaches moved their camp, the women built a dome-shaped hut, called a wickiup, for their family.

moccasins, and the following spring a ritual would be made of his first haircut. Each of these events, and hundreds of others, were social occasions with much singing, dancing, and feasting for friends and relatives. These ceremonies were part of Apache religion.

Cochise was taught Apache religious beliefs as soon as he was old enough to understand them. Through fables told by his parents, he came to know the Apache god, Usen, as well as White Painted Woman and Child of the Water; the Mountain Spirits; and the force called Power that raged before the universe was created and that was contained in all things.

Power was in everything, but it was also possible for Usen to award a gift of Power to an individual, giving him special skills and foresight. Cochise received many gifts of Power, and the Apaches believed that it was these gifts that allowed him to be a successful warrior and leader.

The Apaches believed in many kinds of Power—some good and some bad—and felt that these forces were in constant conflict. This idea explained the enemies in their life and the need to struggle to survive in a region that although very beautiful, presented constant challenges.

Kind beings known as the Mountain Spirits were thought to have lived in the caves of Cochise's homeland. The Apaches believed that these spirits were special protectors and could help with important ceremonies. Any undertaking would be much less prosperous without their assistance. Thus, the Apaches felt a strong connection to their home mountains. To leave them meant to be without the Mountain Spirits.

Although the Apaches stayed near the Mountain Spirits, they moved around quite often within their home territory. The women and children packed up the family's belongings each time the Apaches set up a new camp, and the women built the family's wickiup—a small

Three Apache women display their handiwork. Making baskets, preparing animal hides, and gathering wood were women's tasks, but often children of both sexes helped their mother with their daily work.

dome-shaped hut constructed with sticks and covered with brush or animal hides.

Apache women were responsible for most of the daily chores that kept their families healthy and happy in their ranchería. Children helped their mother as she gathered wood, made baskets for carrying things, and prepared animal skins. The skins were used for blankets and for clothing—breechcloths for the men and shirts and skirts for the women. Although Cochise would not be expected to cook or clean as an adult, working with his mother during his childhood taught him a valuable lesson. He learned never to take a woman's contribution to the family for granted.

When he was free from work, Cochise played games with the other children in the ranchería. Cochise had a younger sister and at least two younger brothers, Juan and Coyuntura, all of whom remained close to him later in his life. Their mother watched all of them carefully as they played, but she kept the closest eye on her eldest son. It was her job to teach him good manners and consideration for others. When he appeared to be too confident, she taught him humility. If he got into trouble, she put a stop to it quickly. He was never allowed to swear or pick on smaller children. Nor could he steal, no matter how trivial the item, or eat another family's food without an invitation. A Chiricahua Apache later described the moral training of a leader's son:

> More pains are taken with such children: they are kept out of mischief. They should not resent things easily. . . . Quarreling should be beneath them. But, above all, the child is taught respect. He was told, don't steal from your friends. Don't be unkind to your playmates. If you are kind now, when you become a man you will love your fellow men.

Although it was rare for Apache parents to punish their children, Cochise's mother and father were undoubtedly quite strict and expected obedience. They hoped that with early guidance he would grow up to be not only a strong fighter but a compassionate man who would care for the less fortunate members of the band—a combination of qualities that would make him a powerful leader.

Around the age of seven or eight, Apache boys were separated from the girls. Their fathers and other male relatives taught them how to use a bow and arrow and began to counsel them in the ways of a warrior. They learned to hunt small animals, and their games became rougher and more competitive than when they were younger. With the other boys, Cochise wrestled, raced, and hid among the rocks and trees, pretending to ambush imaginary enemies.

As Apache boys became stronger, their training became more serious. Cochise learned physical endurance by bathing in ice-covered streams, going for long periods without water, and running long distances. By the time they were adults, most Apache men and women could travel up to 75 miles on foot in a day. They considered this ability a basic skill necessary for survival in a dangerous world.

Because independence was also important to survival, Cochise's father taught him to find his way alone in the countryside. Cochise learned the habits of every animal that lived in the desert; he became adept at hiding in the rocks or under a small bush on the open plain; and he practiced finding water by going to a high peak and looking for green foliage.

The Apaches considered mental discipline every bit as important as physical discipline. In time, Cochise memorized the location of every rock, tree, and hole in Chiricahua territory. He developed patience and self-control by stalking deer, the skin of which was of great value to the Apaches but which was a most difficult animal to hunt. Sometimes, if a herd of deer was grazing in the open, a warrior would be forced to spend hours crawling on the ground behind weeds just to get close to it. Although this kind of hunting could be frustrating, it helped a boy develop stealth, which would come in handy later when he went on raids.

All Apaches trained their children hard, knowing they would need many skills to survive. But because Cochise was the son of a chief, he was often made an example

An assortment of weapons used by Chiricahua Apaches in both ceremony and combat, including a dance shield and spear, a wrist guard, a bow and two arrows, and a pipe tomahawk. Even after firearms became available, the Chiricahuas continued to train their youth to use traditional instruments of war.

for others. By 14 he was ready to begin the final phase of his warrior training, which occurred for most Apache boys at 17 or 18. At this time he became a *dikohe*, or apprentice warrior, and was given a different name. He was called Goci, later spelled Cochise, which means "the strength in wood." As a dikohe, Cochise was assigned to a war leader who helped him perfect his skill with the traditional Apache weapons: bow and arrow, lance, knife, and war club. The war leader was also responsible for explaining the Apache philosophies of warfare and raiding.

An Apache's goal in a raid was to steal possessions—cattle, food, clothing—while putting himself and his fellow warriors at as little risk as possible. People were killed only when necessary for protection, because deaths would attract attention and could lead to retaliatory attacks. By taking precautions to hide themselves, Apache warriors were sometimes able to raid a Mexican ranch without even waking the owners.

The purpose of war, on the other hand, was to kill enemies. Before Americans arrived in Apache territory in the mid-19th century, war was almost always waged to avenge deaths and was considered an important family obligation. Nevertheless, even on a mission of war, caution was essential. The Apaches planned large-scale attacks only rarely. Usually, they used guerrilla warfare tactics and only fought when they were sure they could win. Hiding along canyons and in forests, the Apaches preferred to ambush their victims, striking with the element of surprise in their favor.

In the final phase of his training, when Cochise heard that a raid or war party was being organized, he could volunteer to go along. While away from the camp, he was expected to cook, tend the horses, and stand guard. The older warriors watched him carefully. If a dikohe showed signs of dishonesty or cowardice during his first four raids, he would be labeled unreliable for the rest of his life. But Cochise proved himself to be brave and resourceful—confident but not reckless or disobedient. After four raids he attained warrior status, probably by his midteens, and was considered equal to older men. He could express his own views in council, even when they differed from the leader's, and he could marry, although he chose to wait until several years later.

As Cochise was becoming a warrior, relations between the Spanish and the Apaches were deteriorating. The Mexican revolution, which began in 1810, forced Spain to divert troops and resources away from the presidios to southern Mexico. The soldiers who were left in charge of feeding and disciplining the Apaches were poorly paid and unwilling to work very hard. Money for rations (food allowances) was gone as well, so the Indians started spending more and more time in their own territories.

By the time Mexico won its independence from Spain in 1821, it was clear that instead of becoming dependent on Spanish provisions, the Apaches had become stronger and more self-sufficient during the peace. Many leaders were now experts on Mexican military strategies, and some could even read and write Spanish. Cochise later described the period saying, "After many years the Spanish soldiers were driven away and the Mexicans ruled the land. With these, little wars came, but we were now a strong people and did not fear them."

For Cochise, the Mexican revolution had come at an ideal time. He had had the good fortune to receive his training during a period of relative security, and the "little wars" that followed allowed him to demonstrate his abilities as a warrior. In the years to come he would have many opportunities to earn the respect and experience that would later make him a chief.

A drawing from Harper's
New Monthly, *July 1858, of a
Mexican hacienda, or ranch.
After Mexico discontinued is-
suing rations to the Indians,
the Apaches once again began
raiding haciendas and large
settlements.*

3

THE MEXICAN WARS

After Mexico gained its independence from Spain, the presidios were allowed to close completely and the Apaches could no longer expect rations. Many had continued to hunt and gather food in the wild in the 1820s, but these resources had become scarce. Out of economic necessity, as well as a 200-year history of hostility toward the Mexicans, raiding again became a way of life for the Chiricahua Apaches. Isolated Mexican ranches, called haciendas, were hit constantly, and with military protection at a premium, even good-sized settlements were frequently attacked.

By this time, Cochise had grown to become a distinguished young warrior. He stood out, both literally and figuratively, among his peers. At more than 5 feet and 10 inches tall, he towered over the average Apache, who was at least 5 inches shorter. Cochise had also developed superior fighting skills, and his close association with famed chief Pisago Cabezón added to his power and influence. Now, by going on raids and bringing home large quantities of cattle, horses, and food and occasionally taking captives to trade back for other items, Cochise would gain further prestige among his people.

In an effort to control the Apaches and stop the raiding, the two Mexican states bordering Apache territory—

Sonora and Chihuahua—tried a variety of strategies. Sometimes they signed peace treaties, but because they could rarely fulfill the promises they made to provide the Indians with rations, these treaties failed. Besides, Apache bands operated independently of one another, so a treaty signed by one band was in no way binding on the others.

After a series of successful attacks on Apache rancherías in 1832, Sonora persuaded 29 Chiricahua, Mimbreno, and Nednhi leaders to sign a treaty. Each of the three top chiefs agreed to take responsibility for keeping peace within a particular zone. It was an innovative idea, but this treaty failed as well because it offered the Indians very little in return. After a brief reprieve, the raids began again.

The most drastic strategy for dealing with the Apaches was to exterminate the entire tribe. Both Mexican states posted scalp bounties—as much as 100 pesos for an Apache warrior, 50 for a woman, and 25 for a child. Although the money attracted scalp hunters by the score, this strategy backfired as well. Every time an Apache was killed, the victim's relatives took it upon themselves to avenge the death, which meant more attacks. This complicated cycle of peace and war was only worsened by the frequently changing positions of Sonora and Chihuahua.

In 1837, the stage was set for an incident called the Johnson affair, which would be remembered as one of the most notorious events in Apache history. John Johnson came to Mexico hoping to make a living—one way or another. Like many other Americans scattered throughout the territory at the time, he tried mining for gold and copper. Then he tried trading by buying stolen goods from the Apaches and selling them back to the Mexicans. But it was hard to make a profit.

When Escalante y Arvizu, the governor of Sonora, asked Johnson to track down a herd of mules stolen by

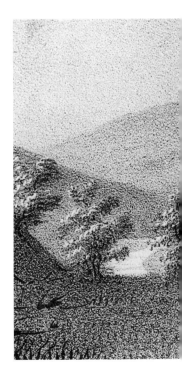

the Apaches, he took the job. His pay would be half of everything he recovered, plus the bounty on any scalps he brought back. With 17 fellow Americans, 5 Mexicans, and a pack train of mules loaded down with provisions, Johnson started north.

Two weeks later, Johnson found two Apache rancherías outside the Santa Rita copper mine in present-day New Mexico—a group of Mimbrenos under Juan José Compá and a group of Nednhis under Juan Diego Compá. He made his camp nearby and pretended to have many goods to trade. Both Apache chiefs had met Johnson before and trusted him.

After a couple of days of friendly talks, the Apaches came to Johnson's camp intending to trade. Johnson offered them food and drink to distract them and then lit a small cannon he had hidden behind some boxes. The air filled with flying metal, wounding many of the Indians, and in the confusion the Americans killed them

An 1848 view of Santa Rita, New Mexico Territory, where John Johnson slaughtered 20 Apaches after luring them into his camp with the promise of trade.

with their shotguns. Twenty Apaches died, including Juan José Compá and Juan Diego Compá.

Johnson left the area quickly for Janos, Chihuahua, where he presented the governor with a report on his "battle with 80 Apaches." He made no mention of the cannon. A captive he brought back told the true story, but it was supressed by the Sonora governor, who had hired Johnson in the first place and did not want to be disgraced. Johnson was paid for his scalps, and the mules were never found.

The Johnson affair had an important effect on early Apache-American relations. Mangas Coloradas, a powerful leader with widespread influence, replaced Juan José Compá as chief of the Mimbrenos. His name, which means "red sleeves" in Spanish, perhaps referred to the splattered blood of his victims. He led several devastating attacks to avenge the deaths at Santa Rita, and eventually the copper mines were forced to shut down.

During this time, Cochise married Mangas Coloradas's daughter, Dos-teh-seh, whose name means "something at the campfire already cooked." She would remain his principal wife for the rest of his life, strengthening his ties to Mangas and the Mimbrenos. According to Apache custom, an Apache warrior was expected to live with his wife's family. But Cochise was considered too important to his people to lose to marriage, so he returned with Dos-teh-seh to the Chiricahuas. A few years later, in 1842, she gave birth to his first son, Taza.

Although Cochise was not present during the Johnson massacre, he participated in the revenge wars that forced the copper mines to close. To avenge these attacks, a group of mercenaries was hired to track down and kill the Apaches. The owner of the Santa Rita copper mines was wealthy and headed a group of businessmen who called themselves the Society to Make War. These men wanted the Apaches stopped and were willing to pay for it. With their support, the governor of Chihuahua established a private army to fight the Indians. James Kirker, another unscrupulous American, was hired to lead it.

Kirker was willing to fight for whichever side paid the most. He was known to kill Mexican peasants and take their scalps, which he would cash in as Apache. The governor, fully aware of Kirker's ruthless behavior, felt that he was the perfect man to lead a band of mercenaries. Indeed, with a well-equipped force composed of American fur trappers, traders, and Delaware and Shawnee Indians, Kirker hunted the Apaches with gusto. But he could never stop them entirely, and eventually he left the area.

Over the next five years, the Mexicans came to know and fear many of the Apache leaders. Pisago Cabezón, Mangas Coloradas, a Chiricahua war leader named Miguel Narbona, and two Chiricahua leaders named Relles and Yrigóllen were the ones most closely associated with Cochise.

Although the Apaches proved themselves to be a fierce enemy, they began to consider peace in 1846. Many Apache lives had been lost, and some of the Indians longed for the days when they had drawn rations and battles were rare. Talks began at the San Buenaventura presidio, commanded by Ensign Carlos Cásares, an honest, sympathetic officer who hoped to create a treaty that would make a lasting difference for both sides.

Cásares called in the Chiricahua chiefs one by one, telling them that he wished to put the past aside and give peace another try. His sincerity won the Indians' trust, and slowly more and more warriors came to him with their families. Cásares warned them that he would issue no rations until all captives had been released, and the Indians complied. Happy with his success, Cásares wrote to the commanding general of Chihuahua:

It is necessary to treat the Indians with gentleness and prudence, never lacking in both. It is also necessary to sustain them so that they comply religiously with the rules, at the same time punishing vigorously those who continue hostilities.

It was a more reasonable policy than most, but unfortunately Cásares would never see the results he hoped for. While Cásares was soliciting the Indians' trust, the governor of Chihuahua, José María Irigoyen, called on James Kirker to help "pressure" the Apaches into making peace.

Kirker was not popular with the Mexican military. Although they knew he was feared by the Apaches, his dishonest methods sometimes created more problems than they solved. When he heard that Kirker was back, the commanding general wrote to Irigoyen: "I do require that [Kirker's men] do not trample on the law nor kill pacified Indians." A copy of his letter was forwarded to Kirker himself, but by then the damage had been done.

On July 1, 1846, Kirker had set out with some 40 men for Galeana, a small frontier town in northern Chihuahua. According to the report he wrote later, he met a group of Mexicans there who were on their way to attack the Indians living at the San Buenaventura presidio. They wanted revenge for past wrongs, and Kirker was happy to assist them.

What followed was a bloodbath that made even the Johnson affair appear trivial. The Apaches living peacefully at San Buenaventura were invited to a feast, where they were given large quantities of whiskey. In the early morning, Kirker and his men, along with the citizens of Galeana, killed the Indians in their sleep. Virtually all were slaughtered—a total of 130 men, women, and children—and their scalps mounted on poles. Referring to the massacre, Mangas Coloradas later said: "My people

This photograph, taken on glass in about 1856, is the only known portrait of James Kirker. An infamous mercenary, Kirker reputedly killed and scalped Mexican peasants in order to collect the bounty that the Mexican state of Sonora offered for an Apache scalp.

drank and became intoxicated. They were lying asleep, when a party of Mexicans came in and beat out their brains with clubs."

Some of the dead were Mimbrenos, some were Nednhis, but most were Chiricahuas. Cochise lost many friends and family members, including Pisago Cabezón and Relles. He was deeply affected by the massacre. For all his raiding, he had probably never even thought of committing so horrible an act. His feelings of hatred and disgust for Mexicans and whites took on a new fierceness. In the inevitable revenge attack that followed, he rose in status among the Chiricahuas, becoming leader of his local group.

For the next few years Cochise's closest associates would be the most militant of Apache leaders: Mangas Coloradas and Miguel Narbona. As a boy, Miguel had spent 10 years as a Mexican captive before he finally escaped at the age of 18. Back with the Chiricahuas, he became a particularly wild and daring warrior with a thirst for Mexican blood. Fighting beside Miguel, Cochise saw almost continuous action. And then one day in June 1848, he, too, was taken captive.

Miguel Narbona and Cochise had just stolen a herd of cattle from a ranch near Fronteras, a small town in northern Sonora, where Cochise often went throughout his life. As the two Apache leaders and their warriors were heading back to the mountains, a group of Mexicans ambushed them, killing two warriors and wounding several others. Miguel and Cochise, with a large band of warriors, appeared at Fronteras early the next morning. Terrified townspeople watched from the church tower as the two warriors took five Mexicans captive and rode out of town.

The next day, a brave Mexican man volunteered to talk to the Apaches. The warriors decided to ransom their captives rather than kill them, but this decision left the previous deaths unavenged. They returned later to attack the presidio at Fronteras, and there Cochise was taken prisoner. He was led to a blacksmith and put in irons, where he remained for six weeks.

Those six weeks were a tense time for the citizens of Fronteras. The Chiricahuas made their camp a scant five miles away and watched while a small military garrison arrived to protect the town. It was clear to the military commander that the Indians were just waiting for an opportunity to take captives whom they could exchange for Cochise. But as usual with the Mexican army, supplies and morale were so low that his men were hardly up to stopping them.

As the weeks passed, farmers stopped working their fields for fear of being taken by the Apaches. Then, when Miguel Narbona moved his camp to within a mile of Fronteras, all traffic ceased completely. At last, when the Mexicans were out of food, a party of 23 soldiers left the fort for provisions and were promptly attacked; all were either killed or captured by the Apaches. Two days later, on August 11, a deal was struck. The Chiricahuas gave up 11 men—a Mexican officer, 4 soldiers, and 6 civilians—in exchange for Cochise, a clear demonstration of his importance to the band.

Although the Mexicans knew better than to treat him badly, Cochise could not forget his imprisonment. Captivity was a humiliation for any Apache, but for Cochise it was an experience not to be repeated—under any circumstances. He would never allow himself to be taken prisoner again.

The town of Fronteras never forgot the experience, either. In fact, later that summer, most of the citizens abandoned their homes and moved to a town called Bacoachi, where they hoped they would be well protected.

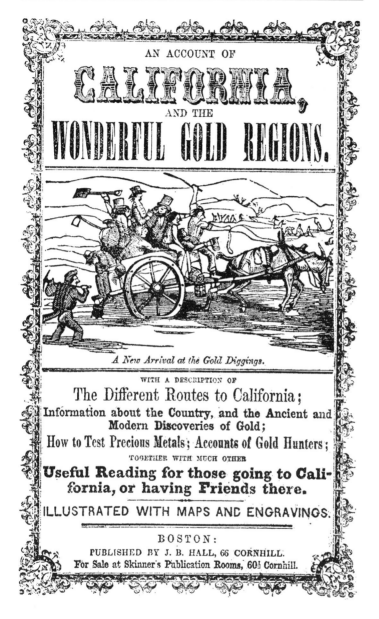

AN ACCOUNT OF

CALIFORNIA,

AND THE

WONDERFUL GOLD REGIONS.

A New Arrival at the Gold Diggings.

WITH A DESCRIPTION OF

The Different Routes to California;

Information about the Country, and the Ancient and
Modern Discoveries of Gold;

How to Test Precious Metals; Accounts of Gold Hunters;

TOGETHER WITH MUCH OTHER

Useful Reading for those going to California, or having Friends there.

ILLUSTRATED WITH MAPS AND ENGRAVINGS.

BOSTON:

PUBLISHED BY J. B. HALL, 66 CORNHILL.
For Sale at Skinner's Publication Rooms, 60½ Cornhill.

Citizens of both the United States and Mexico were drawn to California in 1849 by the promise of gold. Those who left northern Mexico looked forward to living safe from the Apaches as well as to striking it rich.

At nearby Santa Cruz, the situation was no better. On September 8, 1848, a band of Apaches attacked the town, taking 70 cattle and killing 10 horses and 3 mules.

The Apaches had a master plan. Northern Sonora had once been unadulterated Apache territory, and the Indians were now trying to drive the Mexicans out. When there were finally no more cattle to steal, they burned houses and killed any Mexican unlucky enough to come in contact with them. More than mere raiding, these attacks were acts of outright war—a war the Apaches appeared to be winning.

Between April 1849 and April 1850, more than 2,000 citizens abandoned their homes in northern Mexico and migrated to California, drawn by gold and by the promise of a life safe from the Apaches. In July 1850, the new Sonora governor, José de Aguilar, wrote to authorities in the capital of Mexico:

> The frontier is deserted, the prosperity lost, and the lands which had been cultivated reflect only the shadow of what they had been and the graves of many victims sacrificed to the fury of the savages.

For the Apaches in general, and Cochise in particular, it was a glorious time. Cochise had the confidence and respect of his people and the satisfaction of knowing that they were living extremely well. But there were bigger challenges ahead. Before long, a new enemy would make its presence felt in the Southwest.

An 1847 lithograph by Kelloggs and Thayer depicting the storming of the bishop's palace in Monterrey, Mexico, which fell to the Americans in September 1846. Two years later, after Mexico's defeat, the United States acquired Texas and a large piece of northern Mexico as well as the responsibility for policing the Apaches who lived there.

4

A NEW ENEMY

In 1846, Mexico and the United States went to war over territory that is now the state of Texas. When the Americans won the war two years later, the Treaty of Guadalupe Hidalgo awarded them not only Texas but also a large piece of northern Mexico, much of which was Apache homeland. By taking the land, the United States became responsible for the Indians who lived there. The federal government agreed to keep the Apaches from raiding in Mexico, to forbid American citizens from buying stolen Mexican goods, and to return any Mexicans taken captive by the Apaches.

However, the treaty's stipulations were more complicated than they appeared. The Americans had nowhere near enough military power in the Southwest to keep the promises they made to the Mexicans. The Apaches continued to raid in Mexico, as they had for centuries. In fact, because of the American war, Mexico had grown even weaker and more vulnerable to Apache attacks. Feeling that the newcomers had done them a favor, the Apaches' first impression of the Americans was a positive one.

The relationship between Mexico and the United States, with the Apaches in the middle, was further complicated when the United States acquired another piece of Mexican territory through the Gadsden Purchase, ratified in 1854. The international border was moved farther south, and the Mexican army was prohibited from crossing it to pursue the raiding Indians.

When the Chiricahuas became aware of this agreement, they took full advantage of it by crossing the border to raid and then returning to find sanctuary in the United States. Already suffering greatly from Apache attacks, the frustrated Mexicans soon began to feel that the Americans were actually supporting the Indians. They officially accused the Americans of giving the Indians arms and ammunition and then buying the goods the Indians stole.

Whether or not these accusations were true, the U.S. government was forced to take action. Officials in Washington decided on a strategy that combined force and diplomacy: More military personnel were stationed in the area, and in 1855, Dr. Michael Steck was appointed Indian agent to all the southwestern tribes by the U.S. Bureau of Indian Affairs.

Steck was an honest, sympathetic man, and for the most part he treated the Indians well. He began his job by traveling through the region and meeting with leaders from various Apache bands. (He would meet Cochise three years later, in 1858.) In each location, Steck made every effort to establish good relations. He distributed presents, and although he knew full well that the expanding frontier would eventually mean unforeseeable changes for the Indians, he told them of his sincere desire to see the Americans and the Apaches coexist peacefully.

Because these encounters were so cordial, the Apaches allowed Steck to pass through their country unharmed. As American miners and settlers came into the region, they, too, were left alone. But for the Mexicans, the situation was entirely different. Steck reiterated the need for the Apaches to stop raiding, but to most Apaches the

A group of White Mountain Apaches, photographed in 1886. This Western band of Apaches traditionally lived in what is now east-central Arizona. When this territory was acquired by the United States in 1854, the U.S. military was faced with preventing White Mountain Apaches from crossing the border to raid haciendas.

request made no sense. They could not understand why the Americans would protect the Mexicans when they had just been at war with them, and they most certainly did not accept Steck's claim that they were obligated to obey him.

For the Chiricahuas, the first half of the 1850s had been an especially prosperous time. There were few Americans in their territory, and raiding in Mexico was easier than ever, although not without risks. In 1851, three of the Chiricahuas' principal leaders were killed during forays into Mexico. One of these was Yrigóllen, who had been the dominant Chiricahua leader in the 1840s.

Also at this time, other leaders, such as Miguel Narbona, were growing older and losing influence. By 1855, Cochise had emerged as war leader of the entire Chiricahua band. There was no vote, but rather the change happened gradually. In the words of a Chiricahua warrior, "Ability in war and wisdom make the leader. . . . The leader is not chosen, he is just recognized."

In 1857, when it became clear to the United States that raiding would continue, the U.S. military finally began a serious effort to control the Apaches. Led by Colonel R. C. Bonneville, the campaign was aimed primarily at the White Mountain Apaches, though some Chiricahuas were also affected. Hoping to avoid a full-scale war, most of the bands in the area responded by retreating south into Mexico.

Ironically, the Mexicans then decided that it was in their best interest to induce the Apaches to stay. Several frontier towns, such as Janos and Fronteras, offered to make peace. Their rationale was very simple: Although the Mexicans had little hope of controlling the Apaches, they believed that the Indians would raid in the United States if they made their home in Mexico.

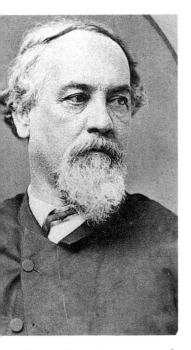

Ignacio Pesqueira, governor of Sonora, was out of town when an urgent message arrived from Fronteras requesting rations for the Chiricahuas. Fearing that his people would soon starve, Cochise left Mexico for southeastern Arizona.

By June 1857, there were between 300 and 400 Indians—mostly Chihennes—living at Janos and receiving rations. Both Mangas Coloradas and Cochise had opposed peace up to that time, but then, in July, Mangas brought his Mimbrenos to Janos. Cochise and his people followed in August.

Soon after the Chiricahuas arrived, the Indians at Janos began to get sick and die. Although their disease was never identified, it is generally believed that the Mexicans poisoned the Indians' rations, hoping to do away with as many of them as possible while they had the chance. As soon as he became aware of the sickness, Cochise told his people to pack their possessions. But for some 60 Chiricahuas it was too late.

Cochise held a council with his top warriors to decide what to do next. With the American military on the offensive, it seemed prudent to remain in Mexico, and a couple of weeks later Cochise approached Fronteras, looking for a peace settlement. As a good-faith gesture, he even returned a captive taken during a raid. Nevertheless, the peace negotiations proceeded slowly. Finally, Cochise could wait no longer. His people were sick and needed food. Although an official treaty had not yet been signed, he brought some 680 Chiricahuas to Fronteras in late September.

The size of the band overwhelmed Captain Gabriel García, the military commander at the town, who barely had enough food for his own men. García sent an urgent request for assistance to Sonora governor Ignacio Pesqueira, but Pesqueira was out of town. Finally, a treaty was drawn up. It was so full of regulations for the Apaches to follow that it is doubtful Cochise would have agreed to it. As it happened, he had already tired of waiting and had returned to the mountains so that his people could gather acorns and berries. The risk posed by the U.S.

military was not serious enough for him to allow his people to starve while he waited to negotiate.

Although the American threat did not last long (eventually, Bonneville was ordered back to his base in what is now New Mexico), Cochise attempted peace at Fronteras again and again over the next year. Because the effect the Americans would have was still basically unknown, perhaps he felt his people would have a better chance of surviving in Mexico, where at least the threat was familiar. The Mexicans were indeed up to their old tricks—treachery and murder.

In July 1858, Fronteras officials invited a group of Chiricahuas to a feast at the town, sedated them with whiskey, and then, when they were drunk, slaughtered them. The death toll consisted of 3 local leaders, 23 warriors, and 10 women. Although it was the same ploy used by Kirker in 1846, the Chiricahuas had not suspected trouble. The Indians had indeed been at peace with Fronteras at various times during the previous 12 years. Betrayed by Fronteras for the last time, Cochise sent a messenger to Mangas Coloradas asking him to join in an Apache attack on the town. It was a full-scale battle, involving some 200 warriors. When it was over, the two Apache bands returned to their separate territories.

Knowing that he could not afford to have enemies on both sides of the border, Cochise decided to make a truce with the Americans. In December 1858, he had his first official meeting with Steck, impressing the agent with his willingness to live in harmony with white settlers. Steck noted in his report that Cochise had allowed the Butterfield Overland Mail Company to build stations in his territory and that travelers had been permitted to pass through unharmed. To encourage this "good behavior," Steck gave Cochise presents, including several head of cattle, blankets, colored cloth, and 200 brass kettles.

Merejildo Grijalva, who escaped from Apache captivity in 1859, once again crossed paths with Cochise at Fort Bowie in 1873. The chief refused to greet the former captive until he was punished for his disloyalty to the Chiricahuas. But after striking Grijalva two or three times with his whip, Cochise gave him a friendly hug and talked of old times.

Over the next year, Cochise's Chiricahuas raided in Mexico but did nothing to keep the Butterfield stages from going about their business. There were occasional lapses (Apache warriors were free to make decisions independent of their leader), but on more than one occasion, Cochise went so far as to return horses and cattle stolen by his men.

In one such case, early in the summer of 1859, Cochise had just returned from Sonora when he found out that a group of warriors had taken 80 horses and mules belonging to the Sonora Exploring and Mining Company in Arizona Territory. According to Merejildo Grijalva, a Mexican captive who belonged to Miguel Narbona, Chiricahua warriors "had strict orders from Cochise never to lay hands on anybody or anything within the boundary of the United States." Grijalva said that when Cochise found out about the raid, he was so angry that he demanded the stock be returned and even killed a warrior who refused to comply.

The Chiricahuas spent the rest of the summer in the upper Chiricahua Mountains gathering acorns and piñon nuts for winter. When they returned to Apache Pass in October, Steck paid Cochise another visit. He reported that he saw about 400 Indians, who were "very friendly and gratified for their presents." He also said that Cochise "promised to watch over the interest of the Overland Mail and travellers upon the great thoroughfare to California that passes directly through his country." Satisfied that good relations between the Apaches and the Americans would continue, Steck returned to his agency in present-day New Mexico. But as soon as he left, the new peace started to break down.

In late November 1859, Cochise led a group of Chiricahuas in a raid on an American's ranch located about 30 miles below the border. They took some mules,

but the owner chased them back into the United States and killed three warriors. Cochise rarely misjudged such situations, and the death of the warriors upset him.

The peace continued to deteriorate. In January 1860, a Butterfield station employee named John Wilson killed a captive Mexican boy, who belonged to Cochise, supposedly in self-defense. The Chiricahuas attacked the station to avenge the death.

Then, in the summer of 1860, Mangas Coloradas went alone on a friendly visit to Pinos Altos, a mining camp in his territory. His warriors had pleaded with him not to go, and their fears were proved correct. The miners tied Mangas to a tree and whipped him. It was not a

A view of the mining camp at Pinos Altos, New Mexico. When Mangas Coloradas made a friendly visit to the camp in the interest of keeping the peace, the miners tied him to a tree and whipped him unmercifully. Such incidents caused relations between Apaches and whites to quickly deteriorate, paving the way for the Cochise Wars.

prudent thing to do to an Apache leader, and the men responsible were later made to pay for it.

In the weeks that followed, the Americans in the region began to feel that their life was in danger. Miners at Tubac, a small settlement about 100 miles from Apache Pass, wrote to Steck:

> Friendly Indians at Apache Pass [have] given intimations of extensive preparations for a total extermination of the Overland Mail line through their country, to be followed by a descent upon the settlements.

Although this rumor was probably based more on paranoia than truth (the Apaches had not attacked an American settlement in several years), it indicates that the Americans no longer trusted the Apaches, especially the Chiricahuas.

Soon every hostile incident involving Apaches was blamed on Cochise's people, whether they were guilty or not. While Cochise continued to return stolen animals, the Americans began to complain that the animals were too few or "not of sufficiently good quality." For an Apache chief to take the trouble to return any animals at all was an unusual gesture. Offended at the Americans' lack of respect and annoyed that Steck had provided "presents" only twice a year, Cochise became less tenacious in enforcing his restrictions on raiding in the United States.

December 1860 and January 1861 passed in relative quiet at Apache Pass. Cochise and his people were camped in their favorite winter home in the mountains. It was there that Butterfield employee James Wallace arranged a meeting between Cochise and Lieutenant Bascom, who had come to retrieve the boy taken captive from John Ward's ranch. At that point, Cochise was still willing to make peace with the Americans. Bascom's actions were to change his mind.

5

A DECADE OF REVENGE

In February 1861, the relationship between the Chiricahuas and the Americans was already strained and much too delicate to withstand the events of the Bascom affair. Some historians say that the trust established by Indian agent Steck was tenuous from the beginning and would have collapsed eventually anyway. But others believe that Cochise did not want a full-scale war with the Americans and would have continued to compromise and negotiate for peace.

Although it is impossible to know just what role the Cut the Tent affair played in breaking down relations with the Apaches, it is evident that afterward there was no longer any hope of the Chiricahuas and the Americans living together peacefully. Cochise had been very close to his brother Coyuntura, and losing him would have been a terrible blow under any circumstances. That his brother was killed treacherously and that he himself had done everything he could to get his brother back—but failed—made the loss almost unbearable.

In the months that followed, Cochise was consumed with grief, and his faith in his own Power was badly shaken. In only a few short years, the newcomers had changed the Apaches' way of life forever. As chief of the Chiricahuas, Cochise felt this weight more than anyone.

After the Cut the Tent affair, Cochise joined Mangas Coloradas in a campaign to drive the Americans out of Apache territory. Their warriors, who were sent out to ambush wagon trains and to raid ranches, showed no mercy when they encountered whites.

He had controlled his anger and resentment in an effort to achieve security for his people. Now the Americans would see the full extent of his hatred. Thus, he set out to cause the Americans as much harm as possible.

The newcomers were now officially considered enemies. Joining Mangas Coloradas, who was still more than a little upset over being whipped by the miners, Cochise began a campaign to drive the Americans out of his territory once and for all. He set up camp in a mountain stronghold and from there sent small groups of warriors out to loot and kill. Whether they were ambushing a wagon train or raiding an isolated ranch, these men showed no mercy. They tortured and killed the men, took women and children captive, and either stole or burned all property they encountered.

By the summer of 1861, most American ranches, mines, and small settlements in the territory that is now Arizona had been abandoned, and traffic through the territory was virtually at a standstill. Even the American military was intimidated. The Apaches were extremely well adept at fighting in their homeland. They knew every trail and spring for hundreds of miles; they could communicate over wide areas using smoke signals; and their ability to hide behind only a cactus or a rock meant they could surprise American soldiers anywhere, anytime.

Arizona Territory was a grim and desolate place for American soldiers. One wrote in his diary that he had "passed many human bones along the road." To pursue the Apaches in this open country was a risk few soldiers wanted to take. In fact, most believed that their only chance of surviving was to stay indoors in large settlements such as Tucson, where they would at least have cover with which to defend themselves.

Although the majority of the Americans in the area in 1861 were desperately afraid of the Apaches, there were

A view of Tucson in 1852, from a watercolor by James Russell Bartlett. Arizona was desolate and dangerous territory in the 1860s, and large settlements such as Tucson appeared to offer the only safety from Cochise's warriors.

a few exceptions. In July 1861, seven former employees of the Butterfield Overland Mail Company, led by Freeman Thomas, made a brave attempt to deliver the mail to California. The men were experienced frontiersmen, but even they were no match for the Apaches.

In the evening on their second day out, they were surprised by a band of more than 100 warriors, including both Cochise and Mangas Coloradas. Thomas responded quickly, ordering his men to drive their wagon up a small hill above the road. When they reached the top, they took their guns, ammunition, food, and water and sent the wagon back down, hoping the Apaches would take it and leave them alone. But the Indians wanted blood, not a wagon. The next morning, they began firing at the Americans, who had built a breastwork of stone on the hill.

The shooting lasted almost two days, but eventually all seven Butterfield men were killed. A short time later, two Americans discovered the scene, and their description of it was published in the *San Francisco Evening Bulletin* on September 7, 1861:

> All about this wall [where the Americans had taken cover] the ground was strewn with battered bullets. Every rock and stone within many yards, which could have partially secreted an Indian, had bullets lying near. One small tree, some 150 yards from the wall, had the marks of eleven balls in it.

Later, Mangas Coloradas showed admiration for these white men. He told one American officer that if his own warriors were to show as much bravery as those seven who had died in the hills, "he could whip the world." He also admitted that the whites had killed 25 Apache warriors and crippled many more, a very serious loss in Apache terms.

That the Indians were willing to lose so many men to kill a handful of American mail employees shows a shift in their military strategy. What had started as raiding was now war, and they were willing to fight to the finish.

While the Americans in present-day Arizona were busy defending themselves against the Apaches, the rest of the United States was engaged in an even bigger crisis—the Civil War. Although most of the fighting in the Civil War took place in the Southeast, the military officers in Apache territory were ordered to abandon their forts and go east to the Rio Grande in the summer of 1861. Their mission was to defend the Southwest against a Confederate attack.

When the Apaches saw them leaving, they thought that they had at last driven the Americans away. It appeared to be a glorious victory, and the Indians celebrated with much feasting and dancing. This atmo-

Confederate colonel John Robert Baylor, in an 1858 drawing. After he arrived in Arizona Territory and pronounced himself military governor, Baylor ordered his men to kill all adult Indians and to sell the children.

phere of celebration was not to last long, however. Confederate forces led by Colonel John Robert Baylor overcame the Union forces at the Rio Grande and settled in Santa Fe.

After pronouncing himself "military governor of the Territory of Arizona," Baylor sent orders to his guard at Pinos Altos in March 1862, in which he informed them of the Confederacy's policy for dealing with Indians:

> The Congress of the Confederate States has passed a law declaring extermination to all hostile Indians. You will therefore use all means to persuade the Apaches or any tribe to come in for the purpose of making peace, and when you get them together kill all the grown Indians and take the children prisoners and sell them to defray the expense of killing the Indians. . . . I look to you for success against these cursed pests who have already murdered over 100 men in this Territory.

Despite his determination, Baylor was no more experienced in fighting the Apaches than the Union soldiers had been. His men caused some trouble for Cochise's Chiricahuas, but for the most part the Apaches were able to avoid costly skirmishes with the Confederates. Then, in May, Baylor's stay in the Southwest ended. He had already taken a tremendous beating from Colorado Union forces when he heard that a column of 1,800 Union volunteers was on its way from California. He retreated back to the South. (Later, Confederate president Jefferson Davis denied having any knowledge of his "law" to exterminate Indians, and the colonel's career was essentially ruined.)

The California Column headed to the territory of Arizona was led by Brigadier General James Henry Carleton. His mission was to drive the Confederates out of the Southwest and to reoccupy the abandoned federal military forts. It was also his intention to subdue the

Apaches so that Americans could continue to settle the territory. To achieve this goal, he would first have to get his men through Apache Pass.

But the Indians got word of the approaching soldiers. Believing that the men's primary mission was to fight the Apaches, Cochise and Mangas Coloradas organized an attack. The California Column was the largest group of soldiers the two chiefs had ever seen. Knowing that they would be outnumbered, they planned their attack carefully, hoping, as usual, that the element of surprise would give them the advantage. By the time the first division of the column approached Apache Pass, Indian scouts had been watching it for several days. The party consisted of 122 men and 11 supply wagons, and the Indians could see that the men were tired and thirsty.

Calling on his fellow chiefs to assist him, Cochise had brought more than 500 warriors to Apache Pass, perhaps the largest Apache group ever assembled for war. The warriors hid in the mountains and even took the time to build a breastwork shield out of rocks, which was unusual for the Apaches, who preferred not to draw attention to their location. Secure in their positions, they watched as the American soldiers came through the pass.

According to Captain Thomas Roberts, who led the first division through the pass, the Indians allowed his men to reach the abandoned stage station and then attacked the wagon train that followed. There was some shooting, but only a few men on each side were hit. Because the station was about 600 yards from the spring, Roberts knew he would have to risk another attack or his men and animals would die of thirst. A few hours later, he began the trip up the narrow canyon and fell right into the Apache ambush.

Using the high-quality guns and large supply of ammunition they had obtained during the last year of

This 12-pound mountain howitzer, manufactured in 1853, saw action in the Southwest, and many others of its kind were used in the Mexican War, the Civil War, and the Indian wars. The Apaches first experienced the effects of a mountain howitzer in 1862, when the California Column destroyed their fortifications in the hills above Apache Pass. Accustomed to fighting with small firearms and bows and arrows, they were left shocked by the cannon blast.

raiding, Cochise's warriors began firing at the soldiers from both sides of the pass. When the Americans fired back, their bullets bounced harmlessly off the stone breastwork. It was clear to Roberts that he would have to do something extraordinary to make it to the spring. He ordered his men to bring forward two of the wagons. Unbeknownst to the Apaches, the wagons contained mountain howitzers—short cannons designed to shoot upward—weapons the Indians had never seen before. Roberts opened fire, and the cannon shells broke open the Apaches' fortifications. Later, a Chihenne warrior told the story from the Apache point of view:

> [Cochise and Mangas Coloradas] would have had an easy victory had the White Eyes not produced a new and terrible weapon—[a] cannon. Shells crashed into the hill sides upon which they lay concealed, dislodging stone and sending earth crashing down the slopes. The Apaches withdrew, carrying their wounded. The cavalry reached the spring.

The Battle of Apache Pass, as this fight would later be known, lasted for four hours. The Americans lost only two soldiers. It is not known exactly how many Apaches were killed, but one officer said as many as 63. Whatever the number of their casualties, the Apaches had experienced a terrible shock.

After the main battle, Roberts sent five of his men on horses back to alert the rest of the column. The men had not gone far when they were overtaken by 20 Apaches, led by Mangas Coloradas. The chief was shot off his horse with a bullet to his chest, and his warriors abandoned the chase to carry him, now unconscious, back to the camp.

Determined to save his father-in-law's life, Cochise took Mangas to Janos in Mexico. There was a doctor there who was known to be particularly skillful with bullet wounds. As legend has it, Cochise left Mangas in the hands of the doctor, telling him he would have to save the chief if he wanted to save the town of Janos. The wound was very serious, but Mangas did recover.

When Carleton arrived, it was immediately clear to him that controlling the spring at Apache Pass was essential if he were to make the California Trail safe again. He left men behind to build a fort, later named Fort Bowie, to guard the water. He then continued to the Rio Grande and assumed command of the Department of New Mexico.

Although Fort Bowie was not an immediate threat to the Chiricahuas, it represented a turning point for Cochise. Having an American military base in the middle of his territory was a constant reminder of defeat. But he could only stand by and watch as the Americans built the fort, which consisted of four long, low buildings with holes in the walls from which the soldiers could fire their rifles.

Carleton's policy for dealing with the Apaches was not much different than Baylor's. He ordered his men to kill all Indian men wherever they were found. Women and children were to be taken prisoner and shipped east where

Brigadier General Joseph West was in command of the soldiers who killed Mangas Coloradas at Pinos Altos in 1863. The chief had approached the settlement under a white flag, ready to talk peace. His murder, which was considered by the Chiricahuas as the "greatest of wrongs," served only to heighten the Apaches' suspicion of whites and to reinvigorate their hatred of Americans.

they would be put on reservations. Within a year he had rounded up the Mescalero Apaches, who lived to the east of the bands associated with Cochise, and had put them on a reservation with the Navajos, ignoring the fact that the two tribes were enemies. In January 1863, he sent Brigadier General Joseph West to do the same with the Mimbrenos and the Chiricahuas.

Mangas Coloradas was more than 65 years old when he was wounded at Apache Pass. After the wound healed, he would continue to be a leader among his people, but he was no longer as strong and energetic as he used to be. His attitude toward the Americans had changed as well. He began to talk of making peace.

When Mangas returned to his homeland near Pinos Altos, he had hoped to find Indian agent Steck. Instead, he found a group of American soldiers led by Brigadier General West. He decided to try to make a treaty with them. His warriors begged him not to go, but Mangas would not be dissuaded. Carrying a white flag, he approached the military encampment, but the soldiers quickly took him prisoner. Sometime later that night he was shot and killed, supposedly while trying to escape.

The loss of Mangas Coloradas affected all the Apaches deeply, but perhaps no one more than Cochise. Within a period of two years American treachery had taken two of his close friends—his brother and his father-in-law. Mangas's murder stilted any thoughts Cochise might have had of making peace with the Americans. The great chief had been killed after going to the American soldiers unarmed, under a flag of truce. The message was clear: The Americans must never be trusted.

Many of the Mimbreno and Chihenne Apaches joined the Chiricahuas after Mangas's death, but others elected to follow the leaders who succeeded him—Victorio, Nana, Loco (all of whom would one day become well known),

and Mangas's son Luis. Like Mangas, the powerful Chihenne leader Victorio had a strong desire to see his people at peace. In 1865, he made several attempts to negotiate a settlement with Carleton. He asked only for a small piece of land along the Alamosa River in his native territory and even offered to help fight hostile Indians and recover stolen stock. But Carleton refused. Determined to take a hard line with the Indians, the general insisted that the 300 to 400 Apaches following Victorio should join the Mescaleros and Navajos who had been placed on a reservation at Bosque Redondo on the Pecos River. That, Victorio would not allow.

Cochise remained on good terms with Victorio, but he refused to join him in his peace negotiations. He continued to attack and kill Americans at every opportunity. During one of Victorio's meetings with Carleton, the general asked him if he could convince Cochise to agree to a settlement as well. Victorio admitted that it was impossible, saying, "[Cochise] does not wish it and will never be friendly more."

Carleton tried everything he could think of to catch Cochise. One of his most innovative ideas was to organize a special group of Indian fighters called the Arizona Volunteers, made up primarily of white officers and Mexican soldiers. Obsessed with capturing the great Chiricahua leader (and enjoying the glory it would bring), Captain Hiram Washburn led the Volunteers into Cochise's territory in August 1865. But within a month they had virtually given up hope of ever succeeding. They were without adequate arms or supplies, and, reported Washburn, every man had become ill from "eating crude fruit and sleeping on the wet ground without blankets."

Cochise's whereabouts in the late 1860s were a mystery to most Americans, but he continued to make his presence felt by sending out parties of warriors to raid and kill. In fact, these years were the bloodiest, most violent in Arizona history, and most crimes were attributed to the Chiricahuas. Everything written about the Apaches at the time, whether by military officers, the Bureau of Indian Affairs, or frontier newspapers, pronounced Cochise the fiercest, most intelligent Apache chief who ever lived. And in 1868, he was officially named "public enemy number one" by the commanding officer in the district of Tucson. By the end of the decade a grim saying was circulating among the Arizona settlers: "Nobody sees Cochise and lives to tell about it."

6

▼▽▼

MANEUVERING TOWARD
PEACE

It was 1868, and Cochise was the most feared Indian in the Southwest. No American had seen the chief and survived since the Cut the Tent affair about seven years earlier. Off and on during this period of intense Apache attacks, the Butterfield Stage Line continued to run through Apache Pass, but the company suffered enormous losses. Thomas Jeffords, a mail superintendent at the time, finally decided it had suffered enough.

Jeffords had been in the Southwest for about 10 years and had already tried his hand at prospecting and soldiering. He took a job with the Butterfield Company in 1867, and over a period of 18 months, lost 14 drivers to the Chiricahuas. He was nearly ready to quit when he decided to visit the chief personally to see if he could convince him to stop killing the Butterfield men. According to Jeffords, he "located one of [Cochise's] Indians and a camp where he came personally . . . [then] went into his camp alone, fully armed."

In 1868, after seven years of Apache vengeance, mail superintendent Thomas Jeffords walked into Cochise's camp uninvited and requested safe passage for his mail carriers. The friendship that was forged between the two men on that day lived on in Apache legends as well as in American history.

Apache scouts had been watching Jeffords for several days. They could have killed him easily at any time, but as he came closer, Cochise became curious. The chief wavered between thinking that the white man was crazy and wondering whether he might be useful. Jeffords was allowed to ride right into the Chiricahua camp.

Showing no fear whatsoever, Jeffords got off his horse, unbuckled his gun, and handed it to one of the Chiricahua women. Then he walked over to Cochise and sat down beside him. After a few moments of silence, the chief asked Jeffords whether he expected to be allowed to leave alive. Undaunted, the mail superintendent replied in Apache that he believed Cochise to be a brave and honorable man. He had come to talk to him about securing safe passage for his mail carriers through Chiricahua territory. He said he wanted to continue to earn his living working for the Butterfield Company, but in order to do so he would need Cochise's cooperation.

After considering Jeffords's request, the chief responded that he could not comply because military messages were carried in the mail and those messages might be used against the Apaches. Jeffords replied that military messages were always carried by courier, never by stage. The answer made sense, and Cochise accepted that it was true.

Legend has it that Cochise was so amazed at Jeffords's courage in coming to his camp that he agreed to leave the mail riders alone. But whether such a pact was made is not clear. Some historians even dispute that the two met in such a way. Company records show that riders continued to be killed by Apaches after 1868. But perhaps they were not the same riders who reported to Jeffords.

That a friendship was initiated between Cochise and Thomas Jeffords, whom the chief called *shik-isn*, or brother, is well documented. Long after Cochise was gone, the strange friendship he shared with the white frontiersman lived on in Apache legends and American history. It was also the subject of an American novel, *Blood Brother* by Elliot Arnold, and a movie called *Broken Arrow* (1950), starring Jeff Chandler as Cochise and James Stewart as Thomas Jeffords.

Soldiers pose with Indian scouts, circa the 1880s. The U.S. military stepped up its operation in the Southwest in the late 1860s and began using "friendly" Apaches as guides to hunt down the Chiricahuas. By February 1869, Cochise was ready to talk to the Americans about peace.

The two would see each other many times over the next few years, and Jeffords would play an important role in later peace negotiations. By all accounts, the two men remained friendly right up until the chief's death.

As the 1860s came to a close, the American military stepped up its operations in the Southwest and began using "friendly" Apaches as guides. Cochise slowly began to feel he was fighting a losing battle. Under Victorio and Nana, the Chihenne Apaches had been living peacefully in their home territory for some time, although they did not have an official treaty with the Americans. It would take time for Cochise to adjust fully to the idea, but by February 1869, he was at least willing to talk to U.S. officials.

It is hard to overstate the magnitude of this transition for Cochise. As chief of the Chiricahua Apaches, he had upheld a fighting tradition that was literally centuries old. He himself had been at war continually with either the Mexicans or the Americans for almost 50 years. Some of his dearest friends and relatives had been lost in those wars—often because of white men's treachery—and for an Apache, those losses were unforgivable. And yet Cochise had the strength to face the truth: The time had come to put aside his hatred and to secure a lasting peace for his people. It would be their only hope for survival.

Captain Frank Perry, commander of Fort Goodwin, left his base in January 1869 with an Indian guide named Phillippi, who promised to lead him to Cochise. Two weeks later, Cochise allowed Perry and his men to enter his territory and agreed to a conference. It had been exactly eight years since his last official meeting with an American officer—Lieutenant Bascom.

Perry described Cochise as "strongly muscled, with mild, prominent features, [and a] hooked nose" and noted that the chief looked "to be a man that means what he says." Dialogue from his meeting with the reclusive chief was published soon afterward in the *Arizona Miner*:

Cochise: What are you doing here, Captain?

Perry: Come to see you and prospect the country generally.

Cochise: You mean you come to kill me or any of my tribe, that is what all your visits mean to me. I tried the Americans once and they broke the treaty first, the officers I mean, this was at the Pass. If I stop in, I must be treated right, but I don't expect they will do all they say for us. I won't stay at Goodwin, it is no place for Indians. They die after being here for a short time. I lost nearly one hundred of my people in the last year, principally from sickness. The Americans killed a good many. I have not one hundred Indians now. Ten years ago I had 1000. The Americans are everywhere, and we must live in bad places to shun them.

When the conference was over, Perry was allowed to continue on his way. Cochise would make no promises, but it was clear to the captain that the chief had accepted the need for peace. His primary objection to bringing his people to Fort Goodwin appeared to have been the smallpox epidemic there, a concern even Perry could understand.

Over the next few months Cochise considered his options, while his warriors continued to attack Americans and raid settlements. Meanwhile, the Chihennes seemed to be getting close to securing the right to live on their homeland. Through his scouts, Cochise was able to monitor the situation closely.

In July 1869, the superintendent of Indian affairs in New Mexico Territory appointed a new agent to the Southern Apaches—First Lieutenant Charles Drew. By October, Drew had had several meetings with Victorio and Loco, and Cochise's messengers reported that the lieutenant seemed to be treating the Indians well. When the Chihenne leaders explained that they wanted a reservation in their own territory, with the government providing rations, the agent passed their request on to his superiors with his full endorsement.

Drew was awaiting word on this request when Loco received a message from Cochise. If the reservation idea worked, the chief would consider bringing the Chiricahuas to Cañada Alamosa, a New Mexican town later known as Monticello. When Drew heard this, he quickly wrote to the superintendent in New Mexico Territory:

> Cochise . . . the most daring robber and bloodthirsty of the Apaches, had said he would come in and join [Loco] as soon as a treaty was made, but he wished to be satisfied that there is no treachery about it, and that if he comes in he will not be betrayed and killed as his people have been in times past.

But for all his efforts, Drew received no support from his superior officer. It seemed that the army did not believe that the Indians, whom they had been fighting for nine years, could be trusted to stay peacefully on a reservation. And the citizens of Arizona Territory felt no different. So many of them had lost friends and relatives in Apache attacks that they sorely resented the idea of giving the Indians food. In fact, whenever the issue of money came up, it was clear that the citizens were willing to contribute generously to a military campaign but would give nothing to keep the Indians fed.

As the weeks passed, it became clear that Drew was to be denied the means he needed to do his job as agent to the Apaches. For all his good intentions, the government would give him nothing—neither food nor clothing nor approval for the reservation at Cañada Alamosa. It was abundantly clear to Cochise that the agent lacked the power to fulfill his promises, and he was not willing to talk to him under such precarious circumstances.

Between the fall of 1869 and the fall of 1870, the Chiricahuas killed several well-known, wealthy people in their raids, which stimulated the U.S. military to pursue them with renewed energy. The officer in charge, Colonel Thomas Devin, declared himself determined to "kill or capture" the Chiricahua chief and spurred his men on, saying that "the officer who succeeds in destroying [Cochise] will earn not only the highest [citations] from his superior but the gratitude of the people of Arizona as well."

One of those officers, Captain Reuben Bernard, proved to be especially successful. Stationed at Fort Bowie, Bernard hired as his guide Merejildo Grijalva, the Mexican captive who had lived with Cochise in the 1850s, and was able to get deep into the mountains of Chiricahua territory. Over a period of weeks, he trailed Cochise from one camp to another, often coming close enough to engage him in battle.

Determined to kill or capture Cochise, Colonel Thomas Devin assured his soldiers that they would enjoy great rewards as well as the gratitude of Arizona citizens for destroying the Chiricahua chief.

Bernard's persistence was a new experience for Cochise. Avoiding him was hard work, and it meant that his people were forced to move constantly. In early August 1870, Cochise made a move that surprised everyone—officers and civilians alike. He sent his wife, Dos-teh-seh, to distant Fort Mogollon to request a peace conference. Fort Mogollon (later called Fort Thomas and then Fort Apache) was located in Western Apache country and already supported nearly 1,000 Indians. Major John Green met with Cochise on August 30. The meeting took place outside the compound, because Cochise was too afraid of betrayal to go inside.

Green reported that the chief "was very respectful; [Cochise] said he had been fighting the Americans for thirteen years, and was now tired and wanted to sleep. The troops had worried him, killed almost all of his band. He thought we were about even, and would like to come on the reservation."

Cochise's influence as a chief was so great that he was well known even among the Western Apaches, but in the end he did not feel comfortable so far from his homeland and decided not to stay. Green thought that by not blocking Cochise's departure, he had taken the first step in gaining the chief's confidence—not an easy thing to do given the Chiricahuas' distrust of Americans. Clearly, any attempt he might have made to use force, when Cochise had come in under truce, would have been a disaster. Nevertheless, the newspapers in Arizona Territory blasted him for letting the legendary Apache slip through his fingers.

Cochise returned to the Chiricahua Mountains and continued to monitor the situation at Cañada Alamosa. While out scouting for hostile Mescalero Apaches, Agent Drew had got lost in the mountains and died of thirst. His replacement, Lieutenant Argalus Hennisee, was not

Captain Reuben Bernard hired for his guide Merejildo Grijalva, a former captive of the Chiricahuas, and trailed Cochise deep into the mountains, often engaging the Indians in combat and forcing them to continually move their camp.

as warm as Drew, but he had experience as an agent, and eventually the Indians came to trust him. By October 1870, regular rations were being issued, although quantity continued to be a problem. Cochise came to Cañada Alamosa on October 20.

It was the first time Cochise had consented to live on a reservation. Hennisee, careful to treat the chief with respect, listened while Cochise talked of his life, noting that he appeared very tired. Cochise made it clear from the beginning that he would not answer any questions about specific things he had done and would not make a commitment of any kind. Then, after again blaming the Americans for starting the war, he explained that he had come because he had lost so many men in the past few years that he now had more dependents than he could provide for. Finally, he said, "If the government talks straight I want a good peace. I want the truth told. A man has only one mouth and if he won't tell the truth he is put out of the way."

This insistence on truth became a widely recognized aspect of Cochise's character. He seemed to make it a point never to make promises he would not or could not keep and expected others to do the same. In a later conversation with Thomas Jeffords, he added, "A man should never lie. . . . If a man asks you or I a question we do not wish to answer, we could simply say, I don't want to talk about that." That the two men were in agreement on the subject was probably an important factor in their friendship.

Cochise lived quietly at Cañada Alamosa for about six weeks. He spent time getting reacquainted with his relatives among the Chihennes, and he talked with Jeffords, who had recently got in trouble with the reservation authorities for trading whiskey to the Apaches for a mule. In late November, Cochise left the reservation with Hennisee's consent, saying that he intended to bring back more of his people. And true to his word he returned a short time later. To Bernard and some of the other military officers, who strongly believed Cochise's stay at the reservation was only a ruse to put them off guard, the chief's return was a sign of his commitment to peace.

Nevertheless, the atmosphere at Cañada Alamosa was far from stable. After gaining the Indians' trust, Hennisee was replaced as agent by Orlando F. Piper, a very religious

man with almost no experience as an Indian agent. He
did his best to maintain the reservation, but in the end
it proved more than he could handle. One of his first jobs
was to inform the Apaches that the United States
government had decided to move them to Fort Stanton
in Mescalero country.

Although the Chihennes had many relatives among
the Mescaleros, the land east of the Rio Grande was
unfamiliar to them, and they preferred not to go. For
Cochise and the Chiricahuas, Fort Stanton was completely unacceptable. Piper quickly determined that the
order was a disaster and wrote to Nathaniel Pope, the
new superintendent of Indian affairs in New Mexico
Territory.

> It would be like beginning all over—they would resist, flee
> to the mountains. . . . [At Cañada Alamosa they have]
> wood, water, pasture and good soil. If the reservation is
> here there is no reason why they can't be satisfied.

In fact, the move to Fort Stanton was only one of
many problems facing Piper. When he took over, there
were nearly 1,000 Apaches living at the reservation, and
government funds could not even provide enough food
and supplies for half of them. With the future of Cañada
Alamosa up in the air, Cochise decided to return to his
native mountains and await the outcome from a safe
distance. Off the reservation, however, the aging chief
was in the domain of the U.S. military. Conflict was
unavoidable. During the first six months of 1871, there
were many small battles, resulting in losses for both
sides.

Meanwhile, Nathaniel Pope was busy trying to secure
rations, hoping to convince Cochise to return to the
reservation. It was through his efforts that the predica-
ment of New Mexico Territory came to the attention of
Indian Commissioner Ely Samuel Parker, a full-blooded

Iroquois Indian. Parker, who lived in Washington, D.C., wanted to meet Cochise for himself. He wrote back to Pope:

> You are instructed to request the Apache Chief Cochise and such other chiefs of that tribe as you may deem to be a proper person on account of his influence among this tribe to visit this city [to] confer with the Department in regard to the welfare of their people.

For the next year, Superintendent Pope tried to convince Cochise that a trip to Washington would solve

Eskiminzin, posing here with his wife, was the chief of the 150 Aravaipa Apaches who came to live at Camp Grant in 1871. In April of that year, a mob of angry whites from Tucson entered the Indian settlement to avenge the death of four Americans, who were murdered in raids made by other Apache groups. More than 100 Aravaipas, most of whom were women and children, were massacred.

all his problems. He instructed Agent Piper to send out messengers to the chief saying that he would meet with him anywhere, but none could find him. Then, in May, Pope got word that Cochise was in the Dragoon Mountains recuperating from a wound received in Mexico. He urged Piper to hire someone to go to him, admitting that finding the right person would be difficult, "for the trip is a very dangerous one."

Piper had tried to interest Thomas Jeffords in the job months before, but Cochise's friend had not wanted to go. In late May he agreed, for a price of $1,000. Jeffords left on June 7, with two Apache scouts and two Mexicans. Two weeks later he arrived in Cochise's camp.

Cochise listened carefully as Jeffords relayed Pope's offer of rations and the invitation to visit Washington. Although he said "he also desired peace and would be glad if his people were at Cañada Alamosa," in the end he refused. Cochise had heard from his messengers that more than 100 Apaches living north of him at Camp Grant had been brutally murdered—and Jeffords could not deny that the story was true.

Led by a man named Eskiminzin, the Apaches living at Camp Grant were some of the most peaceful Indians in the region. They had come there requesting peace in February 1871 and promptly turned their weapons over to the camp commander, Lieutenant Royal Whitman. Within two months, they had planted a good crop of corn, and Whitman had even hired them to cut hay for the soldiers' horses.

Then, in April, four Americans were killed in a raid near Tucson in Arizona Territory. Although there was no evidence that the Indians at Camp Grant were responsible, they were an easy target for revenge. A mob of angry citizens from Tucson, professing to have followed the killers' trail, arrived at Camp Grant two weeks later.

A group of Tucson citizens outside the Pima County Courthouse. Although the killers responsible for the Camp Grant massacre were brought to trial there, they were found not guilty.

Whitman was warned of the attack the same day, but when he reached the Indians' settlement it had already been burned to the ground. All but a few of the dead were women and children. Said Whitman:

> I found quite a number of women shot while asleep beside their bundles of hay which they had collected to bring in that morning. The wounded who were unable to get away had their brains beaten out with clubs or stones. . . . The bodies were all stripped.

Whitman made a great show of burying the bodies of the dead Indians, and perhaps for this reason, Eskiminzin and the other survivors agreed to rebuild their village and start over again. Whitman also ensured that the Tucson killers, many of whom were wealthy businessmen, were brought to trial. But they were found not guilty, and Whitman's support of the Indians against the whites eventually destroyed his career.

General George Crook, shown here in a photograph from 1888, was considered by most Americans to be the best Indian-fighter in the U.S. Army. By June 1870, he had arrived in Chiricahua territory, ready to do battle with Cochise.

Holed up in the mountains, Cochise heard only that Apaches living in peace had been slaughtered in their beds. Soon he would receive more disquieting news: An officer named General George Crook, whom the Americans considered to be the best Indian-fighter in the U.S. Army, was looking for him.

Crook had arrived in the area in June 1870. In an efficient manner, he interviewed everyone involved with the Indians—citizens, scouts, and other military officers—and proceeded to plan a campaign tailored specifically to hunting Apaches. After only a short time, he decided to concentrate his efforts on Cochise:

> This chief has the reputation of being very smart and an uncompromising enemy to all civilization and has such an influence over the . . . other tribes that their warriors are only too glad to join him in his numerous raids.

The general was so confident that he wrote to the War Department in Washington, "I have not the slightest doubt of my ability to conquer . . . a lasting peace with the Apache race in a comparatively short space of time." And there is little doubt among historians that he would have done just that. But only a month after his arrival, Crook received orders that he would have to suspend operations.

For some time, American officials in Washington had strongly disagreed about how to manage the Indians. The War Department listed the crimes they had committed against Americans and insisted that military force was the only way to end the hostility. But the Bureau of Indian Affairs of the Department of the Interior felt that the Indians should be treated fairly and with compassion. Whenever possible, they pointed out that American treachery was in part responsible for the Indians' aggressive behavior. As horrible as it was, the Camp Grant massacre in the Southwest helped tip the scale in the Indians' favor.

In 1871, President Ulysses S. Grant announced a new "peace policy," and later that year he sent humanitarian Vincent Coyler to establish a fair reservation system for the Apaches. For Cochise, the change in policy and Coyler's arrival in Chiricahua territory came just in time.

7

TREATY WITH THE PRAYING GENERAL

When "peace commissioner" Vincent Coyler arrived in Chiricahua country, there were more than 9,000 American citizens living in Arizona Territory. To them he was about as welcome as a wagonload of rattlesnakes.

Throughout the Southwest, newspaper editors wrote that if Vincent the Good would just leave him alone, famed Indian-fighter General George Crook would have the Apache problem cleaned up in no time. The *Daily New Mexican* called the new peace commissioner an "old philanthropic humbug." The editor of the *Arizona Miner* suggested that citizens should "dump the old devil into the shaft of some mine, and pile rocks upon him until he [was] dead."

Despite these slanderous comments, Coyler did what he had come to do. He traveled the region and met with the Apache leaders, discussing their needs and making changes in the reservation system as he saw fit.

All the while, Agent Piper and Superintendent Pope continued to hunt for Cochise. At last, with Thomas Jeffords acting as go-between, they were able to find the chief and convince him to come to Cañada Alamosa. After hearing about him for nearly a year, Piper met Cochise for the first time on September 28, 1871. He gave the

Invested with the authority to take whatever action he deemed necessary to bring an end to hostilities between whites and Apaches, Brigadier General Oliver Otis Howard determined after he arrived in Arizona Territory that he should "make peace with the warlike Chiricahuas under Cochise."

87

chief a special welcome with extra rations and wrote to
Pope that the legendary Indian was "well pleased with
the reception given him."

But others observed that Cochise was not the happy
Apache that Piper made him out to be. In an interview
conducted by *Las Cruces Borderer*, a Mexican newspaper,
the editor described Cochise as thoughtful and melan-
choly. When the editor asked the chief why he had left
Arizona Territory, he said that he had been allowed "no
rest the past year, that the people of Arizona would give

*The Mescalero Apache reserva-
tion near Tularosa, New
Mexico, in 1893. When U.S. officials tried to remove the
Chiricahuas to the land known
as Tularosa, Cochise left
Cañada Alamosa and returned
to his mountain hideout.*

him no peace," and that his beloved homeland was "bad and everything there pinched him."

When Cochise had been at Cañada Alamosa for less than a month, he got word that the Americans were again planning to move the Indians, this time to land known as Tularosa. At first Cochise appeared willing to go, but as time went on it became clear to Piper that none of the leaders liked the idea. They had many reasons, including that the Tularosa environment—swamplike in summer and very cold in winter—would be unhealthy for their people.

Pope, Piper, and Coyler held a council to discuss the move. For Cochise, it was an opportunity to convince the Americans that the Apaches should be allowed to stay put, in a place where they were at least content. In a speech that would later become famous, he left a clear record of his feelings:

> My blood was on fire, but now I have come into this valley and drunk of these waters and washed myself in them and they have cooled me. . . . I speak straight and do not wish to deceive or be deceived. I want a good, strong and lasting peace. . . . The white people have looked for me long. I am here! What do they want? . . . I am not God. . . . I am no longer rich; I am but a poor man. . . . When I was young I walked all over this country, east and west, and saw no other people than the Apaches. After many summers I walked again and found another race of people had come to take it. . . . The Apaches were once a great nation; they are now but few, and because of this they want to die and so carry their lives on their fingernails.

Pope sympathized with Cochise's position, but he still could not see the situation from the Indian's point of view. Holding fast to his plan, he expected that they would eventually agree to go. But they had already given up their freedom and most of their land. To be separated from their homeland completely would be devastating.

With Pope's consent, Cochise left the reservation 10 days later, supposedly to bring back some Chiricahuas who had remained at large and who were still raiding. But the chief had never agreed to move to Tularosa, and Pope knew that in all probability he would not return. In the end, only 350 out of 1,900 Apaches actually made the move. And by the following year, just as their leaders had predicted, many children had died from Tularosa's "bad waters."

Cochise was back in his mountain hideout by the time a new peace commissioner, Brigadier General Oliver Otis Howard, arrived in Arizona Territory. A former mathematics teacher at the U.S. Military Academy at West Point, Howard had served the Union in the Civil War and had even lost his right arm in battle. When the war ended he was put in charge of the Freedmen's Bureau, an organization designed to help newly liberated slaves. Known as a committed humanitarian and a deeply religious man, Howard was given the authority to do whatever he thought best toward creating a lasting peace with the Apaches.

Like Coyler before him, Howard was greeted with resentment, especially by General Crook, who was told that the other general would outrank him. But Crook's unfriendliness did not deter Howard at all. With his aide of many years, Lieutenant Joseph Sladen, he began a tour of the Apache reservations, meeting both with military officers and Indians.

He arrived at Tularosa in September and was very impressed with Victorio, Loco, and Nana. All three Chihenne leaders had made the trip in spite of their misgivings, demonstrating a very strong commitment to peace. Howard listened carefully to their many concerns and agreed to return them to Cañada Alamosa under one condition: All the Apaches not on reservations had to go there, too, including the Chiricahuas.

*Along with Victorio and Nana,
Loco made the trip to Tularosa,
but only 350 out of 1,900 Apaches followed their leaders to the
new reservation. When Howard
visited the three Chihenne
chiefs, he promised to return
them to Cañada Alamosa only
if all the other Apaches, including the Chiricahuas, agreed to
go there.*

While at Tularosa, Howard hoped to convince Cochise to meet with him, and he let it be known that he wanted to meet with the chief. From several sources, he was told that hiring Thomas Jeffords would be his best chance, and it took Howard little time to find him. Jeffords, whom Howard later described as "a tall, spare man, with reddish

hair and whiskers of considerable length," was pointed
out to him by the owner of the trading post. The general
introduced himself and then proceeded to ask Jeffords if
he would be willing to bring Cochise in for an interview.
Jeffords replied,

> General Howard, Cochise won't come. The man who wants
> to talk to Cochise must go where he is. . . . I will take you
> to Cochise. Will you go there with me, General, without sol-
> diers?

Howard said that he would, if necessary, and after a short
negotiation, Jeffords agreed to act as his guide.

Jeffords prepared for the trip carefully. He began by
enlisting the son of Cochise's brother Coyuntura, Chie,
who was related to the Chihennes by marriage. Jeffords
knew that Chie was a favorite of Cochise's (after his
brother's death, Cochise had raised his nephew himself)
and hoped that his presence would help guarantee the
party safe passage in Chiricahua territory.

The group would also need an interpreter. For this job,
Jeffords also had someone in mind—a warrior named
Ponce, who spoke fluent Spanish. That Ponce was married
to a daughter of Mangas Coloradas's and was therefore
related to Cochise's wife Dos-teh-seh would help as well.
Howard's aide, Sladen, two burly Americans, and a cook
would complete the party.

As payment, Howard bought Chie and Ponce each a
new horse. Ponce decided to leave his horse with his wife,
and according to Howard, the two shared the general's
horse on the trip. Sometimes they rode double. At other
times the general walked and Ponce rode. Howard wrote
that this arrangement "greatly pleased" the Apache, who
was probably surprised at the general's generosity.

Howard and the other men set out on September 19,
1872. Five days later they stopped at Silver City, a small
mining village, because one of the horses had lost a shoe.

The rough miners there were notorious Indian-haters, and trouble was inevitable. Howard was shocked when an angry mob threatened his two Apache guides:

> Nobody [at Silver City] believed in the peace policy, but fortunately there were present several sensible men who helped us to remain through the night without suffering violence.

Although the incident was quickly over, it was a clear demonstration of American prejudice against Indians, and it only strengthened Howard's resolve to help them.

From Silver City, the party headed south into the Pelconcillo Mountains. They were riding along a steep dirt trail when suddenly Chie and Ponce both began to shout at once, "Apache! Apache!" and then, "Cochise Apache!" The general was impressed when they studied the tracks in the dirt and were able to tell him the number of people that had passed and how long ago they had been there. The identity of the band was clear in the tracks because the horses had been wearing deerskin shoes—a practice unique to Cochise's Chiricahuas.

The group followed the tracks for some time and then stopped in a clearing between two mountains, where Chie sent up a series of smoke signals and barked like a coyote. There was an answering bark from a nearby peak, and then Chie ran off. He came back with a scout from Cochise's camp. Through Ponce and Jeffords, who translated Ponce's Spanish into English, the scout told Howard that Cochise was currently living in the Dragoon Mountains. Then he added that the general would not be allowed to meet him with so many men. Although a smaller party would be more vulnerable, Howard did not hesitate to send his cook and the two other Americans back to Fort Bowie. He also took the opportunity to send a note to the commanding officer ordering him not to interfere with his mission.

The next day, the sun was especially intense and the air very dry. The group rode for more than 40 miles to a spring known to their Indian guides. They arrived there only to find that the spring had dried up. Several hours later, when Howard was sure the animals could go no farther, they made it to the Sulphur Springs stage station.

After only a few hours' rest, the party left the station at midnight to cross the Sulphur Springs Valley and arrived at the Dragoon Mountains early the next morning. From there it was another day's ride to the top of a mountain, where Chie sent more smoke signals, and they were finally led into Cochise's stronghold.

Howard looked around in amazement at the natural fortification. The Chiricahuas had made their camp in a small valley containing some 40 acres of grassland. There was a small pond in the middle, and out of the pond flowed a clear spring surrounded by small trees. Towering rocky sandstone cliffs and steep hills bordered the valley on all sides; the only opening was the narrow canyon through which they had come. It was an ideal campsite

These rock formations in the Dragoon Mountains conceal the entranceway to a 40-acre valley where Cochise's people could find water and security.

but one especially good for a band living with the constant threat of attack.

Howard and the others were met by a group of Apache women and children who appeared curious and friendly. But Cochise was not in camp and would not return until the next day. This news was disquieting for the general, who then asked his guides whether Cochise intended to talk to him or kill him. Clearly uneasy, Chie and Ponce had to admit that they did not know.

There was nothing Howard could do but pray that he had made the right decision. He spread out his blanket and prepared for bed, but no sooner had he laid his head on his saddle than a few of the Apache children came and curled up around him. Later, the general said that in that moment he knew there would be peace.

Early the next morning the word spread through the camp: "He is coming." The Indians moved quickly to form a circle and set a folded blanket on the ground to receive their chief. Cochise's brother Juan, whom Howard described as "short, thick-set, and much painted with stripes," arrived first, wearing a "fierce look." Juan embraced Jeffords and was introduced to Howard. Then he began a close inspection of the party's possessions.

A few minutes later, Cochise arrived with his sister; a young woman who was said to be one of his wives; and his youngest son, Naiche, then about 14 years old. Cochise embraced Jeffords. Then he turned to Howard, and Jeffords introduced the chief to the general saying, "This is the man." (It was considered improper to say a chief's name.) Cochise reached out to shake Howard's hand and said, "Buenos días, Señor." Then he gave Ponce and Chie a warm greeting and shook hands with Sladen as well. Howard and Sladen were the first U.S. military officers to be welcomed in Cochise's stronghold.

Always cautious, Cochise spent the next half hour or so questioning Jeffords, Chie, and Ponce about Howard.

He asked Jeffords if Howard and Sladen would tell the truth and "do as they say they will." Jeffords replied, "Well, I don't know, I think they will but I will see that they don't promise too much." From Chie and Ponce, the chief wanted to know everything they had observed about the general—where he came from, his rank, the extent of his authority, and his goals for the meeting. When he was thoroughly satisfied with their answers, Cochise turned to Howard and asked why he had come. Howard told him, "I have come from Washington to meet your people and make peace." Cochise responded,

> Nobody wants peace more than I do. I have done no mischief since I came from Cañada Alamosa, but I am poor, my horses are poor and I have but few, I might have got more by raiding on the Tucson Road, but I did not do it.

Cochise then went on to repeat the history of the Apaches and the treachery they had endured at the hands of the Americans. And Howard, hoping to explain this behavior in a way that would encourage confidence, told Cochise that there were "two parties in the United States—one friendly to the Indians, and the other hostile to them." He went on to say that "the friends of the Indians [are] in power now, with General Grant at the head."

Howard told Cochise of his plan to return the Chihenne Apaches to Cañada Alamosa, where the Chiricahuas could live as well. "I have been there," Cochise replied, "and I like the country. Rather than not have peace I will go and take such of my people as I can, but the move will break my band." Then he asked suddenly, "Why not give me Apache Pass? Give me that and I will protect all the roads. I will see that nobody's property is taken by Indians."

Cochise's shrewd suggestion took Howard by surprise, but he did not dismiss it, saying instead, "Perhaps we could do that." Next, Cochise asked Howard if he would

General Howard's aide, Lieutenant Joseph A. Sladen, circa 1872. While Howard left for Fort Bowie on October 1, 1872, to call for a cease-fire, Sladen stayed in Cochise's camp in the Dragoon Mountains.

be willing to stay until he could bring in his captains, who were out "making a living." The general answered that he would stay as long as necessary to make peace. "It will take ten days," said Cochise.

Messengers were sent out immediately, but Cochise did not want to take the risk that his warriors might be attacked by American soldiers on their way back. He asked Howard to ride to Fort Bowie and inform his troops that a cease-fire was in effect. Howard said that he would gladly send Sladen on this errand, but Cochise reasoned, "The soldiers may not obey Captain [Lieutenant] Sladen. . . . I want you to go. Jeffords and Captain Sladen will stay here."

Again, Howard agreed and requested a guide. At first none of the Apaches seemed willing to take the risk, saying, "There is no peace yet," but then Chie volunteered, and the two left later that day. At Fort Bowie, Howard left orders that "[Indians] may not be fired upon when doing no mischief" and then loaded several mules with supplies and returned to the Dragoons.

On the way back up Cochise's mountain, the general was met by Sladen, Jeffords, and several Apaches, who told him that in his absence their chief had moved the entire camp to a new location where they could "at a moment easily conceal themselves behind boulders and crags." The day before, one of Cochise's raiding parties had killed four American soldiers, and he did not want to take the chance that more soldiers would find them. By the next day, however, it was clear that no soldiers had followed the warriors, and the ranchería was moved back to the stronghold. This incident, like the one at Silver City, only strengthened Howard's devotion to bring peace to both sides.

While Cochise waited for his top warriors to arrive, General Howard and Lieutenant Sladen lived with the Chiricahuas in their camp. During this time, both men observed many interesting things about Cochise and his people. They wrote their observations in journals.

The first day, at Cochise's request, a white flag was posted on a hill overlooking the camp. Sladen was with the Indians below at the time and later remarked that the women and children had clapped their hands when the flag went up and shouted an Apache word that meant "I love the flag of peace."

Throughout his stay, Howard slept only 30 yards away from Cochise's wickiup, and he was amazed at its simplicity. He described it as "a couple of boughs leaned against a scrub oak which had grown near a high rock. . . . Furniture consisted of several buckskins . . . a few blankets that had seen long service, some bows and arrows, a rifle in prime order, and four sets of saddles and horseshoes; also a number of knives, a small tin vessel for coffee, a water bucket, and an . . . earthen water-jar."

Howard also observed that Cochise had an especially high regard for his sister, a woman of about 40. She was often at his side and appeared to give him advice and counsel. She was also given the job of guarding Howard and his possessions at night, a task that she performed most diligently.

The children in the Chiricahua camp continued to be fascinated by the one-armed general, and he was happy to spend time with them as well. He played with the youngest and taught the older children, including Naiche, to write a few words of English. They in turn tried to teach Howard a few words of Apache and laughed loudly at his pronunciation.

After a couple of days, Howard noted that the Indians had no regular mealtimes, eating instead throughout the day, whenever they were hungry. He decided to teach them the three-meal-a-day system practiced by the Americans. At the first such meal, he laid his canvas on the ground and invited the Indians to sit with him, with Cochise at the head of the long circle. After the primary warriors had taken their place, the Apache children crowded into every space, and one even sat on the general's leg, eating from his plate and drinking from his cup. Said Howard of the meal, "The white man's table etiquette was not closely followed."

For the most part, this waiting period was a relaxed and friendly time, but on one occasion, several of the warriors, Cochise among them, drank large quantities of *tiswin*, an alcoholic drink made from the mescal plant. Howard wrote in his journal, "Suddenly I heard sharp screams from Cochise's wife and sister, and I saw them fleeing in terror. . . . He was striking and scolding them, and his voice was loud and harsh." The episode worried Howard. It was a side of the great chief he would have preferred not to have seen. But Jeffords was able to calm Cochise and later acted as if nothing was the matter.

Another incident demonstrated Cochise's sophisticated awareness of diplomatic relations. A wounded warrior arrived at the camp and, according to Sladen, was "kept hidden away among the rocks." The Americans could hear Cochise praying for his recovery, and because Sladen had some medical experience, Howard offered Cochise his aide's services. But Cochise would not consent. His reply was most sensible: "The man was dangerously ill and might die. . . . If he did die my people . . . would think that the Captain [Sladen] had given him bad medicine and they would want to kill him."

Every day, more of Cochise's captains returned from the countryside. Said Sladen,

> Their return was always noticed with some formality. When they rode up they went at once to the stone where Cochise was seated, dismounted and sat down upon the ground. With great deliberation, and without any

Chihuahua, one of Cochise's captains, was an up-and-coming leader in the Chiracahua band. On October 11, 1872, after most of his men had come in from raiding, Cochise held a council and discussed Howard's mission. In the end, the Chiricahuas agreed to peace—but only on their own terms.

demonstration of emotion of any kind, they reported to the
Chief; a short conversation ensued, in an ordinary tone, as
if they had been present all the time, and then they retired
to . . . their own immediate family.

The first captain to come in was Nahilzay, Cochise's
brother-in-law. Although he was the war chief of the
Chiricahuas, he seemed to Howard to favor peace. But
others appeared angry and discontented. There was El
Cautivo, the Captive, who appeared to Sladen to be one
of Cochise's most important advisers; Chato and
Chihuahua, two warriors who would later become well-
known leaders; Geronimo, who 14 years later would be
the last Apache to surrender to the Americans; and a
warrior named Eskinya, Cochise's medicine man and an
influential leader. Cochise's oldest son, Taza, who was
raiding in Sonora, was the only captain not present.

On October 11, 1872, Cochise and his men held a
council. Jeffords advised Howard not to interrupt them,
saying, "They [will] let us know if they want to make
peace." But it was soon clear that the Indians had reached
an agreement and were ready to negotiate. In the end,
the terms of the treaty were simple. The Chiricahuas
would be allowed to retain 55 square miles of their
homeland as a reservation, the U.S. government would
provide them with food and clothing, and, at Cochise's
request, Thomas Jeffords would be appointed agent to
the Chiricahuas. In return, Cochise and his men promised
to stop raiding in the United States, to remain on the
reservation, and to protect the roads against attacks from
other Indians so that all travelers could pass in safety.

When the meeting was over, Howard and Cochise said
good-bye to each other in English, and a short time later
the general and his party left for Tucson.

8

THE CHIRICAHUA RESERVATION

The treaty between Cochise and General Howard was a remarkable achievement for both men and for their people. Howard had been willing to put his very life at stake for peace, and Cochise had overcome his intense distrust of the Americans. Although there was no written agreement, the treaty was taken seriously by both sides. A reservation was established in the Chiricahuas' homeland, where the Indians could live out of danger, and the chief saw to it until the day he died that the area was kept safe for Americans.

Nevertheless, the treaty was extremely controversial from the beginning. Cochise was the first Apache to be granted a reservation in his homeland. He was also the first to be allowed to choose his own agent. Citizens and newspaper editors criticized Howard for having given Cochise everything he asked for. That Jeffords had no prior experience as an agent was a further sticking point.

But the loudest objections of all came from General Crook, who called the treaty "a big joke." In his opinion, the fact that the reservation would border Sonora practically encouraged raiding in Mexico. Furthermore, Howard had promised Cochise that there would be "no intervention" from the U.S. military, another first. To Crook, who believed a peace settlement could work only

Taza, Cochise's eldest son. Under normal circumstances there would be a period of transition after Cochise's death, allowing a warrior to win followers and emerge as the chief. But the traditional Apache way of life had been disrupted, and the great chief realized that his people could not be without leadership for any length of time. Having groomed Taza for the position, Cochise appointed him his successor.

103

after the Apaches had been defeated in battle, the treaty was a mistake, and in the years to come he would do all he could to break it.

As soon as Howard left the Chiricahua stronghold, Cochise began to gather his people from the countryside. Then he had his men place a white flag along the Tucson Road as a sign to travelers that the Apaches were at peace.

It was decided that the reservation headquarters would be located at the Sulphur Springs stage station, and with Howard's help Jeffords immediately went to work securing rations. By October 16, 1872, there were 450 Indians to feed, and more were coming daily.

Jeffords's next move as agent was to send a messenger to Fred Hughes, who ran a supply store at Tularosa, offering him a job as clerk. Hughes accepted, and by November 2 he was living with Jeffords in the small one-room station house. A few days later Hughes met Cochise:

> To show how suspicious the old fellow still was, he came ac-
> companied by about fifty warriors. They made their camp
> about half a mile from the agency, but within sight . . .
> then commenced sauntering up to the . . . building in
> squads of twos and threes. . . . [Then] seeing that every-
> thing was all right they took Jeffords down to where
> Cochise was and he brought him up. . . . [Cochise] took me
> by the hand with both of his, told me he had heard of me
> before and that from this day on he was going to be my
> friend. He kept his word till the day he died.

As soon as his band was accounted for, Cochise sent a messenger to the Nednhis, who were living near Janos, inviting them to his reservation. The Nednhis had always been close to the Chiricahuas, but Cochise probably had another motive for bringing them to Arizona Territory: If they lived in Mexico, he would have no way of keeping them from raiding in the United States, and he wanted to do everything he could to uphold his end of the treaty.

This photograph of Naiche, Cochise's youngest known son, was taken by A. Frank Randall in the spring of 1884. Naiche was said to look very much like his father and was considered to be the best-looking man in the tribe.

As Cochise had promised, Indian raids in the southern parts of present-day Arizona came to a complete stop. But the citizens of Arizona Territory were still skeptical. On November 16, the *Arizona Miner* wrote that Cochise would keep the peace "but not beyond next summer." Later that month, Arizona governor Anson Safford paid the reservation a visit. Although he was convinced that Cochise wanted peace, he warned that "some real or imaginary cause may at any moment set them again on the warpath." Of Jeffords, Safford wrote, "I do not believe any other man living could now manage them, wild as they are."

As people began to realize that the Indians were keeping their word, the Chiricahua Reservation became acceptable to the public. But it was never without problems. With Howard no longer present to use his authority on the Chiricahuas' behalf, it became difficult to get rations. Although Jeffords was unhappy with his superior officer (a man named Herman Bendell, who immediately gave him a lesson on the correct way to fold letters), he communicated with Bendell regularly and insisted that the Chiricahuas receive "what the government promised." For his part, Bendell wrote to the Bureau of Indians Affairs that his budget, which was allotted years before when there were only three reservations, would not cover the cost of maintaining the seven in existence in 1872. Still, nothing changed.

Jeffords was very concerned that the lack of rations would jeopardize the entire treaty. He now had 1,025 Indians to feed, and when he could get no satisfaction from Bendell, he wrote to General Howard in Washington, D.C. Howard immediately wrote to the secretary of the interior, who in turn telegraphed Bendell, "See that Chiricahua Reservation is furnished with all needful supplies. Do not neglect this duty." By this time Bendell was as frustrated as Jeffords was, and a few days later he resigned. Before leaving, however, he delivered to Jeffords 23,000 pounds of corn, 1,820 pounds of coffee, 3,640 pounds of sugar, and 910 pounds of soap and salt.

Strangely, throughout this ordeal Cochise was only slightly upset. To him, broken promises were no surprise, and he was not up to making an issue of it. Within a few months of the treaty, Cochise had become sick and seemed to want only to be left alone in his mountain camp. He knew that if necessary, his people could feed themselves by hunting and gathering and by raiding in Mexico, as they had before.

Although Cochise had agreed to protect the Americans, he had not agreed to stop his war with the Mexicans. It soon became clear that the Chiricahua and Nednhi warriors were using the reservation as a base from which to raid, which only substantiated General Crook's suspicions. Complaints came in regularly from Sonora officials, who went so far as to accuse the Americans of giving the Apaches permission to raid and providing them with arms.

For Crook, the complaints furnished an opportunity to interfere with the Chiricahua Reservation and gain control over Cochise. He did his best to convince officials in Washington, D.C., to let him put a stop to the raiding, but because the peace was working on the American side of the border, they were reluctant to agree. Then Crook tried a new strategy. There was a law, which had been ignored by Jeffords, that all Indians on reservations must show up for a daily roll call. When Crook insisted that the Chiricahuas comply with the law, Jeffords answered that this order could drive the Apaches "to the warpath." But that was exactly what Crook wanted. An Apache revolt would give him the excuse he needed to bring in the military and take over the reservation.

Crook also decided to send two of his men to interview Cochise on the chance that the chief could be induced to say something to incriminate himself in regard to the raiding in Mexico. Jeffords arranged the meeting, and the officers arrived on February 3, 1873. When asked about his understanding of the terms of the treaty, Cochise replied, "The troops were to pass and repass by the road on the reservation the same as ever, according to [what] the emergencies of service might require, but none were to come upon the reservation to live, nor were citizens to do so." About the raiding he said,

> The Mexicans are on one side in this matter and the Americans on another. There are many young people whose parents and relatives have been killed by the Mexicans, and now these young people are liable to go down, from time to time, and do a little damage to the Mexicans. I don't want to lie about this thing; they go but I don't send them.

In the early 1860s, Fort Bowie was raided by the Chiricahuas for its horses, which were worth a great deal in Mexico. But on March 27, 1873, Cochise began to make friendly visits to the fort, each time assuring the officers that he was satisfied with the peace. Ironically, the Chiricahuas who accompanied him usually brought stolen merchandise from Sonora to the trading post located at the fort.

From this interview it was clear to Crook that Cochise did not believe himself to be in violation of the treaty, which made Crook's position more difficult. Reluctantly, he canceled his plans for a military takeover, at least for the time being.

On March 27, 1873, Cochise made his first peaceful visit to Fort Bowie, accompanied by 2 of his wives, his sons Taza and Naiche, and 20 warriors. The primary

purpose of the visit seemed to be to maintain friendly relations with the post. Everyone was excited when Cochise met and embraced the commanding officer, Captain Samuel S. Sumner. He then told the crowd that he was very happy with the peace. After eating lunch at the trading store, the Indians returned to their camp at around three o'clock. On future visits Cochise would agree to have a few drinks with the officers, but he always left before sundown and insisted that his people do the same.

Meanwhile, on the Tularosa reservation, the Chihenne Apaches were growing more discontented by the day. General Howard reluctantly told them that without the Chiricahuas coming along as well, he could not return them to Cañada Alamosa. By the summer of 1873, some of the Chihenne warriors had begun to raid in what is now New Mexico, and when the military pursued them, they came to the Chiricahua Reservation for sanctuary. Their families followed, and soon between 200 and 300 more Indians were in residence.

Against orders, Jeffords gave the displaced Chihennes rations, fearing that if he did not they would be forced to raid in Arizona Territory. Eventually, however, Cochise decided they would have to leave. In their current disposition they were likely to start raiding in Mexico, and as much as he would have liked to have offered them a peaceful home, he felt he could not control them.

In spite of this move, raiding continued to be a problem. The clerk at the Fort Bowie trading post, Al Williamson, later recalled:

> I bought from one Indian, a silver mounted ivory handled pistol that he told me he had killed a Mexican officer in order to get. I saw seven Indians ride up to the store one day, on seven Mexican ponies with silver mounted bridles and saddles. I asked them where they got them and they said Sonora. I have seen squaws come into the store with their babies dressed with under garments trimmed with lace, all obtained in their raids.

Supported by General Crook, the governor of Sonora continued to complain about the raiding through official channels, and by August 1873, non-Indians in the region were up in arms over the Chiricahuas. Earlier, Jeffords had refused to take responsibility for the raiding, making his belief clear that the Mexicans deserved it for all they had done to the Apaches in the past. But when he got word that the federal government would be conducting an official investigation, he went to Cochise to discuss the matter.

Over the next few months, Cochise began to return stolen animals. In November 1873, he decided that to ensure peace he would have to put a stop to the raiding for good. He called a council of his warriors and told them that they must "refrain from raiding in Sonora [or] leave the reservation." It was a bold move for a dying Apache chief, but his warriors obeyed him.

Jeffords and others close to Cochise had known for years that he was sick with some kind of stomach ailment. On the reservation, his health had deteriorated. It soon became clear to those who saw him that the chief of the Chiricahuas was constantly in pain. Tiswin seemed to relieve the pain somewhat, and his drinking became heavier than before. But it could not cure him.

In May 1874, the new superintendent of Indian affairs in New Mexico Territory, Levi Edwin Dudley, paid Cochise an official visit. Dudley had come to discuss moving the Chiricahuas away from their homeland and onto a reservation in what is now New Mexico. It was an unpopular idea with everyone but General Crook. Dudley had come to determine Cochise's opinion on the matter. He said of the meeting:

> The old chief was suffering intensely and I at first thought he would not outlive the night. I found a ready welcome as soon as his son [Taza] explained who I was. . . . I gave him a photograph of General Howard and myself taken together

[and] my introduction to his favor was complete. The picture was frequently examined by the old chief during my stay and always followed by the warmest expression of feelings of affection for the general.

There was a short discussion about relocating the Chiricahuas, but Cochise quickly became "much exhausted." Dudley reported back that he was "still alive but failing rapidly." It was clear that the chief did not wish for his people to move, but he would leave the decision to his successor.

The question of who would lead the Chiricahuas into the future was of concern to Apaches and Americans alike. There were three respected warriors vying for the position— Cochise's eldest son, Taza; the medicine man Eskinya; and Nahilzay, Cochise's brother-in-law. Under different circumstances there would have been a period of transition while the three won followers, until one emerged as the leader. But Cochise knew that his people would need leadership immediately and therefore appointed Taza to succeed him after his death. Like his father, Taza had been groomed to lead, and Cochise secured promises from the others that they would give him their loyalty. Cochise's last act as chief of the Chiricahuas was to tell his people "to forever live at peace" with the Americans.

On the evening of June 7, 1874, Jeffords went to visit Cochise and found him in bed. They talked together quietly, and as Jeffords was about to leave, Cochise asked him, "Do you think you will ever see me alive again?" Always honest, Jeffords answered, "No, I do not think I will. I think that by tomorrow night you will be dead." Cochise nodded and said, "Yes, I think so too—about ten o'clock tomorrow morning." Then he asked, "Do you think we will ever meet again?" This question surprised Jeffords. He replied, "I don't know. What is your opinion about it?" And Cochise admitted, "I have been thinking

Thomas Jeffords at his ranch in 1913. He last saw his good friend on June 7, 1874, the night before the chief passed away. Cochise's last instructions to his people were "to forever live at peace" with the whites and to "always do as [Jeffords] tells them."

a good deal about it while I have been sick here, and I believe we will; good friends will meet again." Cochise died the next morning.

News of the legendary chief's death spread quickly among his people. Fred Hughes reported that the Indians wailed loudly for more than a day, and it was "fearful to listen to." Then, according to Apache tradition, Cochise was prepared for burial. A woman close to him, probably Dos-teh-seh or his sister, washed his body and combed his hair.

Traditionally, only the extended family accompanied a body to its final resting place, but according to Jeffords, the only white man present, most of the Chiricahua band attended Cochise's burial. He later described the scene in detail:

> It is the custom among these Indians when one of their number dies to burn some clothing, blankets, etc. at the grave of the deceased. . . . Upon the death of Cochise I found the whole band had stripped themselves of almost their entire clothing and burnt it at his grave. . . .

[Cochise] was dressed in his best war garments, decorated with war paint and head feathers, and wrapped in a splendid heavy, red, woolen blanket that [an American officer] had given him. He was then placed on his favorite horse . . . [which] was guided to a rough and lonely place among the rocks and chasm in the stronghold, where there was a deep fissure in the cliff. The horse was killed and dropped into the depths; also Cochise's favorite dog. His gun and other arms were then thrown in; and, last, Cochise was lowered with lariats . . . deep [into] the gorge.

Naiche and Geronimo at Fort Bowie before they were sent to a prison in Florida. With their surrender to General Nelson A. Miles in 1886, Chiricahua raiding ended and many of the Indians never again saw their homeland.

Cochise was perhaps the most powerful chief in Apache history and a great stabilizing force in the life of his people. In the years to come they would feel his loss deeply. The Chiricahuas were able to resist the move to the territory of New Mexico. But in 1876, the United States government changed its Indian policy yet again. Officials in Washington decided that it was too expensive to maintain a number of small reservations in the Southwest and also wanted the Indians' land for new settlements. Under the new government policy, known as "consolidation," all the Apaches in the region would be moved to one reservation.

The reservation they selected, San Carlos, was located in the middle of Arizona Territory, where the land is flat, dry, and hot, with few trees and many rattlesnakes. By this time even General Crook opposed the idea of uprooting the Chiricahuas, who were just becoming used to living at peace. But there was nothing anyone could do. In June 1876, only four years after General Howard promised Cochise that his people would be allowed to live on their homeland "forever," a military unit came to move them to San Carlos, breaking the historic treaty.

About two-thirds of the Indians on the Chiricahua Reservation agreed to go, led by Taza, who was determined to live at peace according to his father's wishes. The rest took off for the hills and resumed raiding. It

would be another 10 years before the last of these warriors—a band led by Geronimo and Cochise's son Naiche—would surrender for the final time. At this juncture the majority of the Chiricahua band was sent to a prison in Florida, and from there to Fort Sill, a reservation in what is now Oklahoma, where many died from tuberculosis and other diseases. For most of Cochise's band, the day they left the Chiricahua Reservation was the last time they saw their homeland.

CHRONOLOGY

ca. 1805	Born in present-day southern Arizona
1819	Becomes a *dikohe*, or apprentice warrior
1821	Fights in Apache-Mexican wars
1837	Joins Mangas Coloradas, chief of the Mimbreno Apaches, in avenging the Mimbreno and Nednhis Apaches massacred by John Johnson; marries Dos-teh-seh, Mangas's daughter
1842	Dos-teh-seh gives birth to son Taza
1848	Cochise taken captive by Mexicans at Fronteras, Sonora
1855	Becomes war leader of entire Chiricahua band
1857	Makes peace at Janos and Fronteras; returns to homeland in Arizona Territory
1858	Meets Indian Agent Steck at Apache Pass; Butterfield Company begins service through Apache territory
1861	Cochise loses brother and two nephews in the Cut the Tent affair; makes war on Americans
1862	Leads warriors against Union soldiers in Battle of Apache Pass
1868	Meets Thomas Jeffords
1870	Attempts peace settlement at Fort Mogollon; lives on reservation at Cañada Alamosa for six weeks; returns to Chiricahua Mountains to collect the remainder of his band
1871	Returns to Cañada Alamosa for five months; returns to native mountains
1872	Negotiates treaty with General Howard; moves his people to Chiricahua Reservation
1873	Orders Chiricahua warriors to stop raiding in Mexico
June 8, 1874	Dies on Chiricahua Reservation

FURTHER READING

Ball, Eve. *In the Days of Victorio: Recollections of a Warm Springs Apache*. Tucson: University of Arizona Press, 1970.

Betinez, Jason. *I Fought with Geronimo*. Harrisburg, PA: Stackpole, 1959.

Cole, D. C. *The Chiricahua Apache 1846–1876: From War to Reservation*. Albuquerque: University of New Mexico Press, 1988.

Debo, Angie. *Geronimo: The Man, His Time, His Place*. Norman: University of Oklahoma Press, 1976.

Haley, James L. *Apaches: A History and Culture Portrait*. New York: Doubleday, 1981.

Howard, Oliver Otis. *My Life and Experiences Among Our Hostile Indians*. New York: Da Capo Press, 1972.

Lockwood, Frank C. *The Apache Indians*. Lincoln: University of Nebraska Press, 1987.

Sweeney, Edwin R. *Cochise: Chiricahua Apache Chief*. Norman: University of Oklahoma Press, 1991.

INDEX

ACKNOWLEDGMENT

The author gratefully acknowledges the assistance of Edwin R.
Sweeney, author of the definitive biography *Cochise: Chiricahua Apache
Chief.*

PICTURE CREDITS

MELISSA SCHWARZ is a freelance writer and book editor with a longtime interest in the American Western frontier. She is the author of *Geronimo*, another biography in the Chelsea House series NORTH AMERICAN INDIANS OF ACHIEVEMENT. Ms. Schwarz currently lives in Berkeley, California.

W. DAVID BAIRD is the Howard A. White Professor of History at Pepperdine University in Malibu, California. He holds a Ph.D. from the University of Oklahoma and was formerly on the faculty of history at the University of Arkansas, Fayetteville, and Oklahoma State University. He has served as president of both the Western History Association, a professional organization, and Phi Alpha Theta, the international honor society for students of history. Dr. Baird is also the author of *The Quapaw Indians: A History of the Downstream People* and *Peter Pitchlynn: Chief of the Choctaws* and the editor of *A Creek Warrior of the Confederacy: The Autobiography of Chief G. W. Grayson.*